Greene County
Tennessee

COURT OF PLEAS AND
QUARTER SESSIONS

1826–1827

WPA RECORDS

Heritage Books
2024

HERITAGE BOOKS

AN IMPRINT OF HERITAGE BOOKS, INC.

Books, CDs, and more—Worldwide

For our listing of thousands of titles see our website
at
www.HeritageBooks.com

A Facsimile Reprint
Published 2024 by
HERITAGE BOOKS, INC.
Publishing Division
5810 Ruatan Street
Berwyn Heights, MD 20740

The Tennessee Historical Records Survey
Division of Community Service Programs
Work Projects Administration
1941

International Standard Book Number
Paperbound: 978-0-7884-8863-4

W.P.A. RECORDS

The WPA Records are, for the most part, carbon copies of the original that was typed on onion skin paper during the Depression. Since these records were typed on poor machines by people who did not type in some cases and at the same time, they were read by persons not always sure of the older handwritten materials, the results are often less than perfect.

We have made every attempt to make as clear a copy as can be made from these older papers. Sometimes there are water stains and burned edges around the paper. This is the results of a fire at the home of one of the workers, Mrs. Penelope Allen, who was over most of the project. Sometimes, the index will be misleading in that they index by the middle name when a list of names are given in one family, i.e. "... the children of John Smith are, John, Jr., Mary Warren, and Oscar Sims. The indexer would list a Warren and a Sims in the index, when they should be Smith. Mountain Press has acquired a rather large number of finished and un-finished manuscripts. Many of these latter manuscripts are being typed and index now.

The WPA Records are now very scattered between the Tennessee State Library, various Public and Private Libraries and other collections. Some day, there is a hope that all of these can be collected and stored in one place. In spite of their many mistakes and problems, these are still the most complete collection of Tennessee records found anywhere.

GREENE COUNTY

COURT OF PLEAS & QUARTER SESSION
1826-1827

NEW INDEX

NOTE: Page numbers in this index refer to those of original volume from which this copy was made. These numbers
are carried throughout the copy within parenthesis.

3

t

3

Browning, Benjamin D., 193
Broyles, Jacob, 193
Brumley, David, 237
Bruner, Henry, 171
Buster, William, 238
Bryant, Gideon, 105, 106

Caldwell, Alexander, 233
Caldwell, Andrew, 238, 239,
    240, 265, 266
Caldwell, Rachel, 71
Caldwell, Samuel, 153, 202
Caldwell, Thomas, 202
Callayhan, P.O., 75
Callayhan, Patrick O. 75,81,
    219
Campbell, David, 171, 173, 174
Campbell, Elia, 174
Campbell, James, 292, 293, 298,
    302
Cannon, John, 281
Carder, Elijah, 301, 302
Carter, Abraham, 2, 3, 4, 5,
    6, 8, 9, 10, 11, 12, 13,
    16, 17, 18, 19, 22, 23,
    24, 30, 31, 32, 33, 34,
    35, 36, 37, 38, 39
Carter, Benjamin, 104, 264
Carter, Daniel, Jr. 206, 211,
    212
Carter, Elias, 159
Carter, Hugh, 184
Carter, Jacob, 92, 206, 211,
    237, 266, 274
Carter, Joseph, 25
Carter, Nathan, 248
Carter, Samuel, 193
Carter, William, 298, 302
Casteel, Daniel, 46, 235, 276
Casteel, Edward, 57, 58, 59,
    60, 65, 115
Casteel, Jeremiah, 7, 55, 62,
    101, 147, 301, 202, 203,
    239
Casteel, John, 50, 61, 63, 67,
    159, 269, 274, 276
Conner, Thomas, 216
Cessna, Green K., 258, 304
Chuckey River, 214, 247
Chunn, Joseph S., 253, 304
Clevenger, Richard, 244

(Cont'd)

(Page 1)   State of Tennessee Sc.

At a court of Pleas and Quarter Sessions continued and
held for the County of Greene in the court house in
Greeneville on the fourth Monday being the 24th day of
April in the year of our Lord 1826, were present

Merryman Payne   )
    vs   )
Henry Keller   )   Richard M. Woods a constable of Greene
                         County, returned here into Court an
                         Execution issued by Richard West an
acting Justice of the peace for said County against the
Estate of the Defendant for the sum of Twenty nine dollars
fifty seven cents debts (in South Carolina money) and fifty cents costs recovered by the plaintiff against the defendant before said Justice on the fourth day of February
1826, on which execution said constable has made return
as follows "Search made and no personal property found by
me in my County claimed by Defendant Therefore I have levied on all the rights titles & claims that said Keller has
to the following tracts of Land lying on Lick Creek, One
tract of one hundred and seventy nine acres, one hundred
and thirty acres, one of one hundred and four acres, one of
one hundred acres, one of ninety acres, and one of fifty
acres, one of forty   (P-2)   One of thirty five, one of
twenty four, one of twenty one, one of fifteen and one of
ten acres each more or less including the tract whereon
said Keller now lives and all joining each other and joining the lands of Jones Weems, Abraham Carter and others
14th February 1826. R. M. Woods, Con."

Therefore on motion of the plantiff by John A. Aiken
his attorney, it is considered that all the right, title
claim and demand the said Henry Keller, of in and to the
aforesaid several tracts or parcels of Land, be condemned
to the satisfaction of the recovery aforesaid and that the
same are sufficient thereof to satisfy the recovery aforesaid with the interest and the costs of this motion, be
sold as the law directs.

Merryman Payne)
   vs)
Henry Keller) Richard M. Woods a constable of Greene County returned here into court an execution issued by Richard West an acting Justice of the peace for said county, against the estate of the defendant for the sum of thirty two dollars twenty nine cents debt, and fifty cents costs recovered by the plantiff against the defendant before said Justice on the fourteenth day of February 1826. On which execution said constable has made return as follows "Search made and no personal property found by me in my county claimed by defendant Therefore I have levied on all the rights, titles and claim that said Keller has to the following tracts of Land Lying on Lick Creek, one tract of one hundred and seventy nine acres, one tract of one hundred and thirty acres, one of one hundred and four acres, one of forty one of thirty five, one of twenty four, one of twenty one , one of fifteen, and one of ten acres each more or less, including the tract whereon said Kellar now lives and all (P-3) joining the lands of Jones, Weems, Abraham Carters and others 14th February 1826, R. M. Woods Con. Therefore on motion of the plaintiff by John A. Aiken his attorney, it is considered that all the right, title interest claim and demand of the said Henry Keller of in and to the aforesaid several tracts or parcels of Land, be condemned to the satisfaction of the recovery aforesaid, and that the same or sufficient thereof to satisfy said recovery interest constables cost and costs of this motion be sold as the law directs.

Merryman Payne)
   vs)
Henry Keller) Richard M. Woods constable of Greene County, returned here into Court an Execution issued by Richard West an acting Justice of the Peace for said County, against the estate of the defendant for the sum of Seventy five dollars thirty and one half cents debt and fifty cents costs, recovered by the plaintiff day of February 1826. On which execution said constable has made return as follows "Search made and no personal property found by me in my county claimed by defendant for the sum of Seventy five dollars thirty and one half cents debts and fifty cents costs, recovered by the plaintiff against the defendant before said Justice on the fifteenth day of February 1826. On which execution said constable has made return as follows "Search made and no property found by me in my county claimed by defendant, therefore I have levied on all the rights titles and claims that said Keller has to the following tracts of land lying on Lick Creek, one tract of hundred and seventy nine acres, one of one hundred and thirty acres one of one hundred and four acres, one of one hundred acres, and one of ninety acres, one of fifty

one of forty, one of thirty five, one of twenty four, one
of ten acres one twenty one, one of fifteen, and one of ten
acres each more or less including the tract whereon said
Keller now lives and all joining lands of Jones Weems,
Abraham Carter and others 16th February 1826. R. M. Wood
Const." Therefore on motion of the   (P-4)   plantiff
by John A. Aiken his attorney it is considered that all the
right, title, interest, claim and demand of the said Henry
Keller of in and to the aforesaid several tracts or parcels
of land, be condemned to the satisfaction of the recovery
aforesaid, and that the same are sufficient - thereof to
satisfy said recovery with the interest and costs and costs
of this motion, be sold as the law directs.

Valentine Sevier   )
      vs   )   Silver Debt
Henry Keller   )

                      Richard M. Woods a constable of Greene
                      County, returned here into court, an
Execution issued by Richard West an acting Justice of the
peace for said county against the estate of the defendant
for the sum of Seventy one dollars, fifty eight cents in
Silver Debt, and fifty cents costs recovered by the plaintiff against the defendant before said Justice on the
twenty fourth day of February 1826, on which execution said
constable has made return as follows "Search made and no
personal property found by me in my county claimed by defendant, therefore I have levied on all the rights, titles
and claim that said Kellar has to the following tracts of
Land lying on Lick Creek, One tract of one hundred and
seventy nine acres, one of one hundred and thirty acres,
one of one hundred and four acres, one of one hundred
acres, one of ninety acres, one of fifty, one of thirty
five, one of twenty four, one of twenty one, one of fifteen and one of ten acres each more or less, including
the tract whereon said Keller now lives and all joining
each other and joining the land of Jones Weems, Abraham
Carter and others 27th February 1826. R. M. Woods Cons.
Therefore on motion of the plantiff by John A. Aiken his
attorney it is considered that all the right title, interest
claim and demand of the said Henry Keller   (P-5)   of, in
and to the aforesaid several tracts of parcels of land, be
and the same are hereby condemned to the satisfaction of the
recovery aforesaid, and that the same are sufficient thereof
to satisfy said recovery with interest and costs and costs
of this motion, be sold as the law directs.

Valentine Sevier   )
       vs   )
Henry Keller   )   Richard M. Woods a constable of
                           Greene County, returned here
                           into court an execution issued
by Richard West and acting Justice of the peace for said
County against the estate of the Defendant for the sum
of Sixty five dollars ninety three and one half cents
debt and fifty cents costs recovered by the plaintiff
against the defendant before said Justice on the twenty
fourth day of February 1826, On which execution said
constable has made return as follows "Search made and
no personal property found by me in my county claimed
by Defendant, Therefore I have levied on all the rights
titles & claims that said Kellar has to the following
tracts of Land lying on Lick Creek, one tract of One
hundred and seventy nine acres, one of one hundred and
thirty acres, one of one hundred and four acres, one of
one hundred acres, one of ninety acres, one of fifty
acres, one of forty, one of thirtyfive, one of twenty
four, one of twenty one, one of fifteen and one of ten
acres each more or less, including the tract whereon
said Kellar now lives and all joining each other and
joining the lands of Jones Weems, Abraham Carter and
others. 27th February 1826. R. M. Woods Con.

Therefore on motion of the plaintiff by John A. Aiken
his attorney it is considered that all the right, titles
interest, claim and demand of the said Henry Kellar of
in and to the aforesaid several tracts or parcels of land
be and the same are hereby condemned to the satisfaction
of the recovery aforesaid and that the same are sufficient thereof to satisfy said recovery with the interest
and costs & costs of this motion, be sold as the Law
directs.

(P-6)   Monday 24th April, 1826.

Jones & Greenways   )
       vs   )
Henry Keller   )   Richard M. Woods a constable
                            of Greene County, returned here
                            into court an execution issued
by Richard West an acting Justice of the peace for said
county against the Estate of the defendant for the sum
of fifty five dollars debt and fifty cents costs recovered
by the plantiff against the defendant before said Justice
on the 15th day of February, 1826, On which execution
said constable has made return as follows "Search made
and no personal property found by me in my county claimed
by defendant therefore I have denied on all the rights
& titles that said Keller has to the following tracts

of Land, one of one hundred and seventy nine acres, one of one hundred and thirty, one of one hundred and four one of one hundred, one of ninety, one of fifty, one of forty, one of thirty five, one of twenty four, one of twenty one, one of fifteen and one of ten acres each more or less lying on Lick Creek and on both sides including the tract whereon said Kellar now lives and all joining each other and joining the lands of Jones Weems, Abraham Carter and others, 16th February 1826. R. M. Woods, Con."

Therefore on motion of the plantiff by John A Aiken their attorney it is considered that all the right, title interest, claim and demand of the said Henry Keller of in and to the aforesaid several tracts or parcels of land be and the same are hereby condemned to the satisfaction of the recovery, with the interest, costs and costs of this motion, be   sold as the law directs.

(P-7)   Monday 24th, April 1826

John Ottinger	)	
vs	)	Ca Sa issued by a justice of the
Gilbert Evans	)	peace

The defendant having been arrested by virtue of a Ca. Sa. issued by a Justice of the peace and having given Bond for his appearance at the present court - appeared accordingly and having taken insolvent - Debtors oath - It is ordered that he be discharged and that the plaintiff pay the costs in this behalf expended

John Grymes	)	
vs	)	Ca. Sa. Issued by a Justice
John Ingram	)	of the peace

The defendant having been arrested by virtue of a Ca. Sa. issued by a Justice of the peace and having given Bond for his appearance at the present court - Appeared accordingly and having taken the Insolvent Debtors Oath It is ordered that be discharge and that the plaintiff pay the costs in the behalf expended

Joseph Jones	)
vs	)
Michael Basinger	)

The plantiff by his attorney dismisses his suit and Jeremiah Casteel fer the defendand assumes the costs. Therefore It is considered that the plaintiff recover against the said Jeremiah Casteel his cost by him about his suit in this behalf expended.

(P-8)
Thomas Crutchfield)
vs)
Solomon Rouss)

The plantiff in his proper
person appeared in court and
dismisses his suit and assumes the payment of the costs

Therefore It is considered that the Defendant recover
against the plantiff his costs by him about his Defence
in this behalf expended.

William K. Vance)
vs)
Henry Keller)

Richard M. Woods a constable of
Greene County returned here into
court an execution issued by Richard West esquire and
acting Justice of the peace for said county against the
estate of the Defendant for the sum of thirty eight dollars
and twenty cents Debt and fifty cents costs recovered by
the plantiff against the Defendant before said Justice on
the fourth day of February 1826 on which execution said
constable has made return "Search made and no personal
property found by me in my county claimed by defendant
therefore I have levied on all the rights, titles and
claim that said Keller has to the following tracts of land
lying on Lick Creek, One tract of one hundred and Seventy
nine acres, one of one hundred and thirty acres, one of
one hundred and four acres, one of one hundred acres, one
of ninety acres, one of fifty acres, one of forty, one of
thirty five, one of twenty four, one of twenty one, one
of fifteen and one of ten acres each more or less including the tract whereon said Keller now lives and all joining each other and joining the lands of Jones Weems, Abraham Carter and others. 14th February 1826. R.M.Woods con.

Therefore on motion of the plantiff by John A. Aiken
his attorney It is considered that all the right, title
Interest claim and demand of the said Henry Keller of in
and to the aforesaid several tracts of a parcels of land
be condemned to the satisfaction of the recovery aforesaid
and it is ordered that the same or sufficient thereof to
satisfy said Recovery with Interest costs and costs of the
motion be sold as the law directs.

(P-9)
Jones & Greenway)
vs)
Henry Keller)

Richard M. Woods a constable of
Greene County returned here into

Court an execution issued by Richard West esquire an acting Justice of the peace for said County against the estate of the Defendant for the sum of thirteen Dollars Ninty five and one half cents Debt and fifty cents cost recovered by the plantiff against the Defendant before said Justice on the fifteenth day of February 1826 on which execution said constable has made return "Search made and no personal property found by me in my county claimed by Defendant therefore I have levied on all the rights, titles and claim that said Keller has to the following tracts of land lying on Lick Creek. One tract of one hundred and Seventy nine acres, one of one hundred and four acres, one of one hundred acres, one of ninety, one of fifty, one of forty, one of thirty five, one of Twenty four, one of twenty one, one of fifteen and one of ten acres, each more or less including the tract whereon said Keller now lives and joining each other and joining the lands of Jones Weems, Abraham Carter and others. 16th February 1826. R. M. Woods, Con."

Therefore on motion of the plantiff by John A.Aiken his attorney, It is considered that all the right, title, interest claim and demand of the said Henry Keller of in and to the aforesaid and it is ordered that the same or sufficient thereof to satisfy said Recovery with interest - costs - and the costs of the motion be sold as the law directs.

(P-10)
George Weems)
vs)
Henry Keller)

Richard M. Woods a constable of Greene County returned here into Court an execution issued by William Jones esquire an acting Justice of the peace for said county against the estate of the Defendant for the sum of Twelve Dollars and Twenty four cents debt, recovered by the plantiff against the Defendant before said Justice on the 13th day of February 1826 (with the further sum of fifty cents) on which execution said constable has made return "Search made and no personal property found by me in my county Claimed by Defendant therefore I have levied on all the rights, titles and claim that said Keller has to the following tracts of land lying on Lick Creek - one tract of one hundred and Seventy nine acres, one of one hundred and thirty acres, one of one hundred and four acres, one of one hundred acres, one of ninety acres, one of fifty one of forty, one of thirty five one of twenty four, one of twenty one, one of fifteen, and one of ten acres, each more or less including the tract, whereon said Keller now lives, and all joining each other and joining the

lands of Jones Weems, Abraham Carter and others.
14th February 1826. R. M. Woods Con.

Therefore on motion of the plantiff by John A. Aiken
his attorney, It is considered that all the right, titles
Interest Claim and demand of the said Henry Keller of in
and to the aforesaid several tracts or parcels of land be
condemned to the satisfaction of the recovery aforesaid
and it is ordered that the same or sufficient thereof to
satisfy said Recovery with the Interest, Costs, and the
costs of this motion be sold as the law directs.

(P-11)   Monday April 24th 1826

George Weems   )
      vs   )
Henry Keller   )
                        Richard M. Woods a constable of
                  Greene County returned here into court
an execution issued by William Jones esquire an acting
Justice of the peace for said County against the estate
of the defendant for the sum of nineteen Dollars and twenty
three cents debt and fifty cents cost recovered by the plantiff against the defendant before said Justice on the 13th
day of February 1826 on which execution said constable has
made return "Search made and no personal property found
by me in my county claimed by Defendant, therefore I have
levied on all the rights, titles and claims that said Keller
has to the following tracts of land , One of one hundred
and seventy nine acres, one of one hundred and thirty, one
of one hundred and four, one of one hundred, one of ninety
one of fifty, one of Forty one of thirty five, one of
twenty four, one of twenty one, one of fifteen and one of
Ten acres each, more or less, lying on Lick Creek, and on
both Sides including the tract whereon said Keller now
lives and all joining each other and joining the lands of
Jones Weems, Abraham Carter and others.

     14th February 1826.   R. M. Wood Con."

Therefore on motion of the plantiff by John A. Aiken
his attorney. It is considered that all the right, title,
interest, claim and demand of the said Henry Keller of in
and to the aforesaid tracts of land be condemned to the
satisfaction of the recovery aforesaid, and that the same
or sufficient thereof to satisfy said Recovery with the
interest costs and the costs of this motion be sold as
the law directs -

(P-12)

George Weems)
    vs)   Silver Debt
Henry Keller)

          Richard M. Woods a constable of
Greene County returned here into
Court and execution issued by William Jones esquire an
acting Justice of the peace for said County against the
estate of the Defendant for the sum of eight dollars
and ten cents Debt - in Silver and fifty cents costs, recovered by the plantiff against the defendant before said
Justice on the 13th day of February 1826. On which execution said constable has made return. "Search made and
no property found by me in my county claimed by Defendant
therefore I have levied on all the rights titles and claim
that said Keller has to the following tracts of land lying on Lick Creek, One tract of one hundred and Seventy
nine acres, one of one hundred and thirty, one of one
hundred and four acres, one of one hundred, one of ninety
acres, one of fifty, one of forty, one of thirty five,
one of twenty four, one of twenty one, one of fifteen,
and one of ten acres, each more or less including the
tract whereon said Keller now lives and all joining each
other and joining the lands of Jones Weems, Abraham Carter
and others, 14th February 1826 R. M. Woods Con.

    Therefore on motion of the plantiff by John A. Aiken
his attorney - It is considered that all the right, title,
interest, claim and demand of the said Henry Keller of in
and to the aforesaid several tracts or parcels of land be
condemned to the satisfaction of the Recovery aforesaid
and that the same or sufficient thereof to satisfy said
Recovery with the interest, costs and the costs of the
motion be sold as the law directs -

(P-13)   Monday 24th April 1826

Peter Pitsonbarger)
    vs)
Henry Keller)

          Richard M. Woods a constable
of Greene County return here
into court an execution issued by said Richard West esquire an acting Justice of the peace for said county
against the estate of the Defendant for the sum Thirty
two dollars and thirty cents Debt and fifty cents cost
recovered by the plantiff against the defendants before
said Justice on the 25th day of February 1826. On which
execution said constable has made return "Search made and
no personal property found by me in my county claimed by
defendant, therefore I have levied on all the right, title
claims and claim that the said Keller has to the following

tracts of land lying on Lick Creek, one tract of One hundred and seventy nine acres, one of one hundred and thirty acres, one of one hundred and four acres, one of one hundred acres, one of ninety acres, one of fifty, one of forty, one of thirty five, one of seventy four, one of twenty one, one of fifteen, and one of ten acres, each more or less including the tract whereon said Keller now lives and all joining each other and joining the lands of Jones Weems, Abraham Carter, and others. 27th February 1826. R.M. Woods Con.

Therefore on motion of the plantiff by John A. Aiken his attorney. It is considered that all the right, title, interest claims, and demand of the said Henry Keller of in and to the aforesaid several tracts or parcels of land be condemned to the satisfaction of the recovery aforesaid and that the same or sufficient thereof to satisfy said Recovery with the interest, costs, and the costs of the motion be sold as the law directs.

(P-16)
Valentine Sevier   )
    for the use of   )
    Alexander Henderson)
)
    vs   )
)
Henry Keller   )

Richard M. Woods a constable of Greene County returned here into court an execution issued by Richard West an acting Justice of the peace for said County against the estate of the defendant for the Sum of thirty one dollars and fifty cents Debt and fifty cents costs recovered by the plantiff against the Defendant before said Justice on the 24th February 1826 - On which execution said constable has made return "Search made and no personal property found by me in my county claimed by Defendant, therefore I have levied on all the rights, titles, and claim that said Keller has to the following tracts of land lying on Lick Creek, One tract of one hundred and Seventy nine acres one of one hundred and thirty acres, one of one hundred and four acres, one of one hundred acres, one of ninety acres one of fifty acres, one of forty acres, one of thirty five one of twenty four, one of twenty one, one of fifteen and one of ten acres, each more or less, including the tract whereon said Keller now lives and all joining each other and joining the lands of Jones Weems, Abraham Carter and others 27th February 1826. R. M. Woods, Con.

Therefore on motion of the plantiff by John A. Aiken his attorney, It is considered that all the right, title, interest claim and demand of the said Henry Keller of in

on to the aforesaid several tracts or parcels of land be
condemned to the satisfaction of the recovery aforesaid
and that the same or sufficient thereof to satisfy said
recovery with the Interest costs, and the costs of the
motion be sold as the law directs.

(P-17)   Monday 24th April 1826

Valentine Sevier   )
    Surviving partner   )
    of Deaderick & Sevier   )
    for Alexander Anderson   )
)
        vs   )
)
Henry Keller   )
                        Richard M. Woods a
                        constable of Greene
County returned here into court an execution issued by
Richard West esquire an acting Justice of the peace for
said County against the estate of the Defendant for the
Sum of nine Dollars fifty one and a half cents Debt and
fifty cents cost recovered by the plantiff against the Defendant before said Justice on the 24th day of February
1826 - On which execution said constable has made return
"Search made and no personal property found by me in my
county claimed by Defendant therefore I have levied on all
the rights, titles and claim that said Keller has to the
following tract of land lying on Lick Creek - one tract of
one hundred and seventy nine acres and one of one hundred
and thirty acres, one of one hundred and four acres one of
one hundred acres, one of ninety acres, one of fifty acres,
one of forty acres, one of thirty five, one of twenty four
one of twenty one, one of fifteen and one of ten acres,
each more or less, including the tract whereon said Keller
now lives and all joining each other and joining the lands
of Jones Weems, Abraham Carter and others 27th February
1826.

                        R. W. Woods Con.

    Therefore on motion of the plantiff by John A. Aiken
his attorney, It is considered that all the right, title,
interest, claim and Demand of the said Henry Keller of in
and to the aforesaid several tracts on parcels of land
be condemned to the same or sufficient thereof to satisfy
and recovery with the Interest, costs, and the costs of
this motion be sold as the law directs

(P-18)
Alexander Anderson Assignee   )
    of Hugh Malony   )

vs)
)
Henry Keller)

          Richard M. Woods a constable of Greene County returned here into court an execution issued by Richard West esquire an acting Justice of the peace for said County against the estate of the defendant for the sum of five Dollars seven and one half cents Debt and fifty cents costs recovered by the plantiff against the Defendant before said Justice on the 7th day of March 1826 on which execution said constable has made return "Search made and no personal property found by me in my county claimed by Defendant therefore I have levied on all the rights, title and claims that said Keller has to the following tracts of land lying on Lick Creek. One tract of one hundred and Seventy nine acres, one of one hundred and thirty, one of one hundred and four acres, one of one hundred acres, one of ninety acres, one of fifty, one of forty, one of thirty five, one of twenty four, One of twenty one, one of fifteen and one of ten acres, each more or less including the tract whereon said Keller now lives & all joining each other and joining the lands of Jones Weems, Abraham Carter and others 15th day of March 1826

                    R. M. Woods Con.

    Therefore on motion of the plantiff by John A. Aiken his attorney. It is considered that all the right, title, Claim and Demand of the said Henry Keller of in and to the aforesaid several tracts, or parcel of land be condemned to the satisfaction of the recovery aforesaid and that the same or sufficient thereof to satisfy said recovery with the Interest. Cost, and the costs of this motion be sold as the law directs -

(P-19)   Monday 25th April 1826

Alexander Anderson assignee)
   Hugh Maloney)
)
)
    vs)
)
Henry Keller)

                    Richard M. Woods, a constable of Greene County returned here into court an execution issued by Richard West esquire an acting Justice of the peace for said County against the estate of the Defendant for the Sum of Twenty five Dollars and fifty cents Debt and fifty cents costs recovered by the plantiff against the defendant before said Justice on the 7th day of March 1826.

On which executed said constable has made return "Search
made and no personal property found by me in my county
claimed by Defendant - therefore I have levied on all the
rights, titles and claim that said Keller has to the following tract of land lying on Lick Creek - One tract of
one hundred and seventy nine acres, one of one hundred
and thirty acres, one of one hundred and four acres, one
of one hundred acres, one of ninety acres, one of fifty
one of forty, one thirty five, one of twenty four, one
of twenty one, one of fifteen and one of ten acres, each
more or less including the tract whereon said Keller now
lives, and all joining each other and joining the land
of Jones Weems, Abraham Carter and others.
15th day of March 1826. R. M. Woods, Con.

Therefore on motion of the plantiff by John A. Aiken
his attorney it is considered that all the right, title,
claim and demand of the said Henry Keller of in and to
the aforesaid several tracts or parcels of land be condemned to the satisfaction of the recovery with the Interest - costs and costs of the motion be sold as the law
directs -

(P-22)
Jacob Smith   )
      vs   )
Henry Keller   )   Richard M. Woods a constable of
                        Greene County returned here into
                        court an execution issued by Joseph
Brown esquire an acting Justice of the peace for said
County against the estate of the Defendant for the sum
of Forty five Dollars Debt and Two dollars cost recovered
by the plantiff against the Defendant before M. Lincoln
esquire on the 8th day of April 1826. On which execution
said constable be made return "Search made and no personal property found by me in my County claimed by Defendant therefore I have levied on all the rights, titles and
claim that said Keller has to the following tracts of
land lying on Lick Creek - One tract of one hundred and
seventy nine acres, one tract of one hundred and thirty
acres, one tract of one hundred and four acres, one of
one hundred acres, one of ninety acres, one of fifty
acres, one of forty, one thirty five, one of twenty four
one of twenty one, one of Fifteen and one of ten acres,
each more or less including the tract whereon said Keller
now lives, and all joining each other and joining the
land of Jones Weems, Abraham Carter and others
15th day of March 1826. R. M. Woods, Con.

Therefore on motion of the plantiff by John A. Aiken
his attorney it is considered that all the right, title,
claim and demand of the said Henry Keller of in and to the

aforesaid several tracts or parcels of land be condemned
to the satisfaction of the recovery aforesaid and that
the same or sufficient thereof to satisfy said recovery
with the Interest, costs and the costs of the motion be
sold as the law directs -

(P-23)
James Ross   )
   vs   )
Henry Keller   )   Richard M. Woods a constable of
                 Greene County returned here into
                 Court an execution issued by
Richard West esquire and acting Justice of the peace for
said county against the estate of the Defendant for the
sum of ninety five Dollars and eleven cents Debt and
fifty cents cost recovered by the plantiff against the
defendant before said notice on the 15th day of April
1826 on which execution said constable has made return
"Search made and no personal property found by me in my
county therefore I have levied on all the rights titles
and claim that said Keller has to the following tracts
of land lying on Lick Creek one tract of one hundred and
seventy nine acres, one tract of one hundred and thirty
acres, one tract of one hundred and four acres, one tract
of one hundred acres, one of ninety acres, one of fifty
acres, one of forty, one of thirty five, one of twenty
four, one of twenty one, one of fifteen and one of ten
each more or less, including the tract whereon said Keller
now lives, and all joining each other and joining the
lands of Jones Weems, Abraham Carter and others.
21st April 1826

                        R. M. Woods Con.

Therefore on motion of the plantiff by John A. Aiken, It
is considered that all the Right, Title, Interest, Claim
and demand of the said Henry Keller of in andto the
aforesaid several tracts or parcels of land be condemned
to the Satisfaction of the recovery aforesaid and that
the same or sufficient thereof to satisfy said Recovery
with the Interest, costs, and the costs of this motion
be sold as the law directs.

(P-24)
James Ross   )
   vs   )
Henry Keller   )
                 Richard M. Woods a constable of
                 Greene County returned here into

Court an execution issued by Richard West esquire an
acting Justice of peace for said County against the estate of the Defendant for the Sum of thirty one dollars
and twenty four cents, Debt and fifty cents costs recovered by the plantiff against the Defendant before said
Justice on the 15th day of April 1826, on which execution
said constable has made return "Search made and no personal property found by me in my county claimed by Defendant therefore I have levied on all the rights, titles,
and claim that said Keller has to the following tracts of
land lying on Lick Creek, One tract of one hundred and
Seventy nine acres, one tract of one hundred and thirty
acres, one tract of one hundred and four acres, one of
one hundred acres, one of ninety acres, one of fifty
acres, one of forty, one of fifteen and one of ten acres,
each more or less including the tract whereon said Keller now lives and all joining each other and joining the
land of Jones Weems, Abraham Carter and others.
21st April 1826   R. M. Woods, Con.

Therefore on motion of the plantiff by John A. Aiken
his attorney, It is considered that all the right, title,
claim and demand of the said Henry Keller of in and to
the aforesaid several tracts or parcels of land be condemned to the satisfaction of the recovery aforesaid
and that the same or sufficient thereof to satisfy said
recovery with the Interest costs and the costs of this
motion be sold as the law directs

(P-25)   Monday 24th April 1826

Joseph Carter   )
     vs   )
Henry Keller   )

                John Brothertin a constable of
                Greene County returned here into
Court on execution issued by William Jones esquire an
acting Justice of the peace for said County against the
estate of the Defendant for the sum of forty four Dollars eighteen cents Debt and fifty cents Cost recovered
by the plantiff against the Defendant before said Justice
on the 13th day February 1826. On which execution said
constable has made return "State of Tennessee Greene
County, "Search made and no personally property found
therefore levied on 3 track of land the one whereon he
lives containing 200 or 300 acres, one track of 200 acres
ajoining the said track and one **** acres by warrent
ajoining land of Jacob Saylor and others levied the 15th
February 1826

                John Brothertin, Cost.

Therefore on motion of the plantiff by Seth J.W. Luckey his attorney, It is considered that all the right, title, the aforesaid several tracts or parcels of land be condemned to the satisfaction of the Recovery aforesaid and that the same or sufficient thereof to satisfy said recovery with the Interest costs and the costs of this motion be sold as the law directs

(P-28)   Tuesday 25th April 1826

	Hale Baxter
Joseph Nebinnerg	James Park
Jacob Bible	George Murray
Abraham Bible	Thomas Bailey

good and lawful men of the county of Green who being now here empannelled and sworn to esquire for the State aforesaid and for the body of the county aforesaid received their charge and retired from the Bar.

Jacob Bible a constable was gratified to attend on the above Jury 2 days. Certf. issd.

For sufficient cause shewn - ordered that George Rightsell, Jacob Sailor, Archibald Nelson be excused from further attendance at the present court as Jurors.

Certif. issd (Seal)   Leland Davis appointed a constable
by Jos Davis   to attend on the court in the place
9 Jany. 1827   of Thomas Self, 4 days

John Lane   )
   vs   )   Certio
George Welty   )   Continued by consent

John Kennedy & V. Sevier   )
        vs   )   Cont.
Philip Harmon   )

                              The defendant in his
                              proper person appeared
in court and confessed that he owes the plantiff the sum of one hundred eighteen dollars and ninety two cents - Therefore It is considered that the plantiff recover against the Defendant the aforesaid Sum of one hundred eighteen Dollars and ninety two cents and their costs by them about their Suit in   this behalf expended

(P-29)
John Kennedy & V. Sevier   )
        vs   )   Covenant
Philip Harmon   )

The Defendant in his proper person appeared in court and confeses that he owes the plantiff the Sum of one hundred twenty four Dollars ninety three and one half cents the amount of the principal and Interest on the writing obligatory - Therefore It is considered that the plantiff recover against the Defendant the aforesaid sum of one hundred twenty four Dollars ninety three and one half cents according to his confession and their costs by them about there Suit in this behalf expended

(P-30)

John S. Reed)
   vs)
Henry Keller)

      Elliot Rutherford a constable of Groene County returned here into court an execution issued by Joseph Brown esquire and acting Justice of the peace for said county against the estate of the Defendant for the sum of Twenty nine Dollars and fifty nine cents Debt and fifty cents costs recovered by the plantiff against the defendant before William Jones esquire on the 18th day of February 1826, On which no personal property by me in my county therefore I have levied on all the rights, titles and claims that said Henry Keller has to the following tracts of land lying on Lick Creek One tract of one hundred and seventy nine acres, one tract of one hundred and thirty acres, one tract of one hundred and four acres, one of one hundred acres, one of ninety acres, one of fifty acres, one of forty acres, one of thirty five acres, one of twenty one acres one of fifteen and one of ten acres each more or less including the tract whereon said Keller now lives, and all joining each other and joining the land of Jones Weems, Abraham Carter and others - 11th March 1826.

        E. Rutherford Const.

Therefore on motion of the plantiff by James W. Wyly his attorney, It is considered that all the right, title, claim and demand of the said Henry Keller of in and to the aforesaid Several tracts or parcels of land be condemned to the satisfaction of the recovery aforesaid and that the same or sufficient of the recovery aforesaid and that the same or sufficient thereof to satisfy said recovery with the Interest, costs, and the costs of the motion be sold as the law directs

(P-31)   Tuesday 25th April 1826

John S. Reed)
   vs)   United States Money
Henry Keller)

Elliot Rutherford a constable of Greene County returned here into Court an execution issued by Joseph Brown esquire an acting Justice of the peace for said County against the estate of the Defendant for the sum of Seventy Seven Dollars debt and fifty cents cost recovered by the plantiff against the Defendant before William Jones esquire an acting Justice of the peace for said county on the 18th day of February 1826 on which execution said constable has made return "Search made and no personal property found by me in my county therefore I have levied on all the rights, titles and claims that said Henry Keller has to the following tracts of land lying on Lick Creek one tract of one hundred and Seventy nine acres, one tract of one hundred and thirty acres, one tract of one hundred and four acres one of one hundred acres, one of ninety acres, one of fifty acres, one of forty acres, one of thirty five acres, one of twenty four, one of twenty one, one of fifteen and one of ten acres each more or less including the tract whereon said Keller now lives and all joining each other and joining the lands of Jones Weems, Abraham Carter, and others. 11th March 1826

E. Rutherford Const.

Therefore on motion of the plantiff by James W. Wyly his attorney It is considered that all the right titles claim and demand of the said Henry Keller of in and to the aforesaid several tracts of land be condemned to the satisfaction of the recovery aforesaid and that the same or sufficient thereof to satisfy said recovery with the Interest, costs and the costs of this motion be sold as the law directs

(P-32)   Tuesday April 1826

John S. Reed   )
    vs   )
Henry Keller   )

Elliott Rutherford a constable of Greene County returned here into court an execution issued by Thomas Smith esquire an acting Justice of the peace for said County against the estate of the Defendant for the sum of eighty five Dollars Twenty two cents Debt and fifty cents costs recovered by the plantiff against the Defendant before said Justice on the 25th day of March 1826 - On which execution said constable has made return "Search made and no personal property found by me in my County therefore I have levied on all the rights titles and claim that said Henry Keller has to the following tracts of land lying on Lick Creek One tract of one hundred and seventy nine acres, one

tract of one hundred and thirty acres, one tract of one
hundred and four acres, one tract of one hundred acres, one
of ninety acres, one of fifty acres, one of forty acres,
one of thirty five acres, one of twenty four, one of twenty
one, one of fifteen and one of ten acres, each more or less
including the tract whereon said Keller now lives, and all
joining each other and joining the lands of Jones Weems,
Abraham Carter, and others 1st April 1826

       E. Rutherford Const.

  Therefore on motion of the plantiff by James W. Wyly
his attorney It is considered that all the right, title
claim and demand of the said Henry Keller of in and to
the aforesaid several tracts of land be condemned to the
Satisfaction of Recovery aforesaid, and that the same or
sufficient thereof to satisfy said recovery with the Interest costs and the costs of this motion be sold as the
law directs.

(P-33)
John S. Reed   )
  vs   )
Henry Keller   )
      Elliot Rutherford a constable of
      Greene County returned here into
Court an execution issued by Thomas Smith esquire an acting Justice of the peace for said county against the estate of the defendant for the Sum of eighty eight Dollars
and twenty five cents Debt and fifty cents cost recovred
by the plantiff against the Defendant before said Justice
on the 25th day of March 1826, On which execution said
constable has made return "Search made and no personal
property found by me in my county therefore I have levied
on all the rights, titles and claim that said Henry Keller
has to the following tracts of land lying on Lick Creek
One tract of one hundred and seventy nine acres, one of
one hundred and thirty acres, one tract of one hundred
and four acres, one of one hundred acres, one of ninety
acres, one of fifty acres, one of forty acres, one of
thirty five acres, one of twenty four acres, one of twenty
one acres, one of fifteen and one of ten acres each more
or less including the tract whereon said Keller now lives
and all joining each other and joining the land of Jones
Weems Abraham Carter and others.

  1st April 1826.   E. Rutherford Const.

  Therefore on motion of the plantiff by John Kennedy
his attorney It is considered that all the right, title,
claim and demand of the said Henry Keller of in and to
the aforesaid several tracts or parcels of land be

condemned to the satisfaction of the aforesaid and that
the same or sufficient thereof to satisfy said recovery
with the Interest, Costs and the costs of this motion be
sold as the law directs -

(P-34
John S. Reed   )
    vs   )
Henry Keller   )

Elliott Rutherford a constable of
Greene County returned here into
court an execution issued by Thomas Smith esquire an acting Justice of the peace for said County against the estate of the Defendant for the sum of eighty Dollars and
eighteen cents Debt and fifty cents cost recovered by the
plantiff against the Defendant before said Justice on the
25th day of March 1826 on which execution said constable
has made return "Search made and no personal property
found by me in my county therefore I have levied on all
the rights titles and claim that said Henry Keller has to
the following tracts of land lying on Lick Creek one tract
of one hundred and seventy nine acres, one tract of one
hundred and thirty acres, one tract of one hundred and
four acres one of one hundred acres, one of ninety acres
one of fifty acres one of forty acres, one of thirty five
acres one of twenty four acres, one of twenty one acres,
one of fifteen acres, and one of ten acres, each more or
less including the tract whereon said Keller now lives
and all joining each other, and joining the lands of Jones
Weems, Abraham Carter and others 1st April 1826

E. Rutherford Const."

Therefore on motion of the plantiff by John Kennedy
his attorney It is considered that all the right, title,
claim and demand of the said Henry Keller of in and to the
aforesaid several tract or parcels of land and that the
same or sufficient thereof to satisfy said recovery with
Interest, costs, and the costs of this motion be sold as
the law directs

(P-35)
Samuel West   )
    vs   )
Henry Keller   )

James Goss a constable of Greene
County returned into court an execu-
tion issued by John Hardin esquire and acting Justice of the
peace for said County against the estate of the Defendand
for the sum of Seventy four Debt and fifty cents cost recovered by the plantiff against the defendant before said
justice on the 14th day of January last past (1826) on which

execution said constable has made return   "Search made and
no personal property found by me in my county to levy this
execution, therefore I have levied on all the right, title,

interest and claim that said Keller has to the following
tract of land lying on Lick Creek - One tract of one hundred and seventy nine acres, one tract of one hundred and
thirty acres, one tract of one hundred acres, one of ninety acres, one tract of fifty acres, one tract of forty
acres, one tract of thirty five acres, one tract of twenty
four acres one tract of twenty one acres, one tract of
fifteen and one of ten acres each tract more or less including the tract whereon said Keller now lives and all
joining each other and joining the lands of Jones Weems
Abraham Carter and others. 6th day of April 1826

                    Jas. Gass Cost.

     Therefore on motion of the plantiff by James W. Wyly
his attorney It is considered that all the right, title
claim and demand of the said Henry Keller of in and to
the aforesaid several tracts or parcels of land be condemned to the satisfaction of the recovery aforesaid
and that the same or sufficient thereof to satisfy said
recovery with the Interest costs, and the costs of this
motion be sold as the law directs   (P-37) Tuesday
25th April 1826.

Eliakim Cox   )
     vs   )
Henry Keller   )
                    Elliott Rutherford a constable of
                    Green County returned here into
Court an execution issued by William Jones esquire an
acting Justice of the peace for said county against the
estate of the defendant for the sum of twenty two Dollars and twenty seven cents debt and fifty cents cost
the Balance of a Judgment recovered by the plantiff
against the Defendant before said Justice on the 13th
February 1826. On which execution said constable has
made return   "Search made and no personal property
found by me in my County therefore I have levied on
all the right, title, claim that said Henry Keller has
to the following tract of land lying on Lick Creek one
tract of one hundred and seventy nine acres, one of one
hundred and thirty acres, one of one hundred and four
acres, one of one hundred acres, one of ninety acres, one
of fifty acres, one of forty acres, one of thirty five
acres, one of twenty four acres, one of twenty one acres
one of fifteen acres, and one of ten acres each more or

less including the tract whereas said Keller now lives
and all joining each other and joining the land of Jones
Weems, Abraham Carter and others 9th April 1826.

E. Rutherford Const."

Therefore on motion of the plantiff by John Kennedy
his attorney, It is considered that all the right, title,
claim and demand of the said Henry Keller of in and to
the aforesaid several tracts or parcels of land be condemned to the satisfaction of the recovery aforesaid and
that the same or sufficient thereof to satisfy said recovery with the Interest, costs and the costs of this motion
be sold as the law directs.

(P-38)
John Cook   )
    vs   )
Henry Keller   )

Thomas Dodd a constable of Greene
County returned here into court an
execution issued by John Cass esquire an acting Justice
of the peace for said county against the estate of Defendant for the sum of Six Dollars debt and fifty cents
costs recovered by the plantiff against the Defendant before said Justice on the 24th day of April 1826, On which
execution said constable has made return "Search made and
no personal property found by me in my county therefore I
have levied on all the right, titles, and claim that said
Keller has to the following tracts of land lying on Lick
Creek one tract of one hundred and seventy nine acres, one
tract of one hundred and thirty acres, one tract of one
hundred and four acres, one of one hundred acres, one of
ninety acres, one of fifty acres, one of forty acres one
of thirty five acres, one of twenty four one of twenty
one, one of fifteen and one of ten acres, each more or
less including the tract whereon said Keller now lives
and all joining each other and joining the land of Jones
Weems, Abraham Carter and others April 24th 1826

Thos. Dodd Const.

Therefore on motion of the plantiff by James P. Taylor
his attorney It is considered that all the right, title,
claim and Demand of the said Henry Keller of in and to the
aforesaid several tracts or parcels of land be condemned
to the satisfaction of the recovery aforesaid and that the
same or so much thereof as will satisfy said recovery with
the Interest, costs and the costs of this motion be sold
as the law directs

(P-39)
John Haun   )
    vs   )
Henry Keller   )

Thomas Dodd a constable of Greene
County returned here into court
an execution issued by Leonard Starnes esquire an acting Justice of the peace for said county against the estate of the Defendant for the sum of five Dollars sixty
six and one fourth cents recovered by the plantiff against
the Defendant before said Justice on the 10th day of March
1826 on which execution said constable has make return
"Search made no personal property to be found by me in my
county therefore I have levied on all the rights and claims
that said Keller has to the following tracts of land lying
on Lick Creek one track*of one hundred and four acres, one
tract of one hundred and seventy nine acres, one of one
hundred and thirty, one of one hundred and four acres one
of one hundred acres, one of ninety acres, one of fifty
acres, one of forty acres, one of thirty five, one of
Twenty four, one of twenty one, one of fifteen, and one
of ten acres, each more or less, including the track
whereon said Keller now lives and all joining each other
and joining the lands of Jones Weems, Abraham Carter and
others March 11th 1826 returned by me.
*of one hundred and thirty acres, one tract
                        Thomas Dodd constable"

Therefore on motion of the plantiff James P. Taylor
his attorney, It is considered that all the rights, titles, claim and demand of the said Henry Keller of in
and to the aforesaid several tracts or parcels of land
be condemned to the satisfaction of the recovery aforesaid
and that the same or sufficient thereof to satisfy said
recovery with the interest, costs, and the costs of this
motion be sold as the law directs

(P-40)   Tuesday 25th April 1826

And court adjourned until tomorrow morning 9 oclock.

                        A. D. Hale

                        Jesse Kerby

                        R. West

Wednesday 26th Apl. 1826

Court met present

John Baker   ) Certio
vs   ) On motion and cause shewn
Howell Houston &) by affidavit of William Houston
William Houston) this cause is continued until
         the next term of this court.

John Matthews Assgnee)
John Mooncaster   )
vs   ) Appl.
George Bell applt.)

      On motion and cause shewn
      by affidavit of John Matthews
this cause is continued until the next court

State of Tennessee

John Cummings prosr.)
vs   ) T. A. B.
Jacob Rymal   )

     This day came as well the attorney General as the Defendant in his proper person and the Defendant being charged on the Bill of Indictment for plea thereto says that he is guilty in manner and from as charged in the Bill of indictment (P-41) Tuesday 26th April. 1826 and puts himself on the mercy of the court therefore it is considered by the court that the Defendant for such his offence be fined forfeit and pay to the State of Tennessee the sum of twenty five cents and that he pay the costs of this prosecution and thereupon Jacob Rimal Senr. assumed and undertook for the Defendant the payment of the fine and costs aforesaid and agrees that Judgment be entered against him for the same - therefore It is considered that the state of Tennessee recover against the said Jacob Rymal Senr. the fine and costs aforesaid according to his assumpsit -

State of Tennessee

John Cummings prosr.)
vs   )
Jacob Rymal Deft.)

     This day came as well the attorney General as the Defendant in his proper person and the Defendant being charged on the Bill of Indictment for plea thereto says that he is guilty in manner and form as charged in the Bill of indictment and puts himself on the mercy of the court - Therefor It is considered that the Defendant for such his offence be fined and and pay to the state of Tennessee the sum of

Twenty five cents and that he pay the costs of this prosecution - And thereupon came Jacob Rymal Senr. and assumed
and undertook for the defendant the payment of the fine and
costs aforesaid and agrees that Judgment be entered against
him for the same therefore It is considered that the State
of Tennessee recover against the said Jacob Rymal Senr.
the fine and costs aforesaid (P-42)   Wednesday 26th
April 1826 according to his assumpsit -

State of Tennessee

Thomas H. Wilson prosr.   )
       vs   )   T. A. B.
Ironymus Dyche   )
                                    This day came as well
                                    the attorney General as
the Defendant in his proper person and thereupon a Jury
to wit   Daniel Britten, James Mccollam, William Grubbs,
Levi Babb, William Mitchell, George Bell, Ryon Wood,
William Brannon, William Boling, John Malony, John Shields
and James Lowrey who being elected tried and sworn the
truth to speak upon this issue of Traverse upon their
oath do say that the Defendant is guilty in manner and
form as charged in the Bill of Indictment - Therefore It
is considered that the Defendant for such his offence
be fined forfeit and pay to the State of Tennessee the
sum of two Dollars and fifty cents and that he pay the
costs of this prosecution - and thereupon came William
Bales and assumed for and on behalf of the defendant
the payment of the Fine and Costs aforesaid and agrees
that Judgment be entered against him for the same. Therefore It is considered that the State of Tennessee recover
against the said William Bales the fine and Costs aforesaid
according to his assumpsit.

State of Tennessee

Leland Davis prosr.   )
       vs   )   Assault &c.
William Easley   )
                                    This day came as well the
                                    Attorney General as the Defend-
ant in his proper person and the Defendant being charged
on the Bill of indictment for plea thereto says that he is
not guilty in manner (P-43)   and form as charged in
the Bill of Indictment and puts himself on the County and
the Attorney General having done the same - came also a
Jury towit   William Bales, William Trobaugh, Levi Dunn
John Walker, William Likens, Jacob Garrett, John Lauderdale, Dutton Lane, Isaac Fox, Marmaduke Lamb, Jacob Rymal
and Eli Rambo who being elected, tried and sworn well and
truly to try this issue of Traverse upon their Oath do say

that the Defendant is not guilty in manner and form as charged in the Bill of indictment -

And on motion and
for satisfactory reasons
appearing to the Court
It is ordered that Leland
Davis the prosecutor
pay the Costs of this
prosecution -

Samuel Walker)
vs) Appeal
Zachariah Kinnamon Applt)

On motion - Ordered
that the plaintiff give
Security for the costs of this Suit on or before Monday
of the next Court or the same will be dismissed at his
costs ---

State of Tennessee

John Bowman prosr.)
vs) T. A. B.
Leonard Rush)

This day came as well the
attorney General as the De-
fendant in his proper person and thereupon a Jury towit
Charles Dyche, Ironymus Dyche, Emanuel Dyche, Joseph
Brown, Philip Bird, William Lawson, Charles Nichols,
Amos McBride, Charles Love, Isaac Earnest, Thomas Wilson
and Samuel Standfield who being elected tried and sworn
the truth to speak upon   (P-44)   this issue of Traverse upon their Oath do say that the Defendant is guilty
in manner and form as charged in the Bill of Indictment.

And on motion of Defendant
by Attorney a Rule is al-
lowed him to shew cause
why a new Trial should be
granted. Whereupon all and
singular the premises being
seen and by the Court fully
understood - It is considered
that said Rule be made absolute.

And thereupon Leonard Rush acknowledged to owe the
State of Tennessee One hundred Dollars and Churchill
Rush his Surety also acknowledged to owe the State of
Tennessee the Sum of fifty Dollars - Yet upon condition

that if Leonard Rush shall make his personal appearance
at the Court of pleas and quarter Sessions to be held
for the County of Greene in the Court house in Greeneville
on Wednesday next after the fourth Monday in July next
and stand his trial in this prosecution against him and
not depart the Court without leave then the above recognizance to be void otherwise in force -

State of Tennessee)
    vs)   Affray
Eli Rambo)

               This day came as well the
               Attorney General as the Defend-
               ant in his proper person and
thereupon a Jury to wit David Britton, James McCollum,
William Grubbs, Levi Babb, William Mitchell, George Bell,
Ryan Woods, William Boling, James Lowrey, James Lauderdale, John Shields and William Bales who being elected
tried and sworn the truth to speak upon the issue joined
upon their Oath do say that the Defendant is not Guilty
in manner and form as charged in the Bill of Indictment

    And on motion It is ordered that the   (P-45)   Costs
of this prosecution be paid by the Trustee of Greene County ---   Cetife issd.

State of Tennessee

Thomas H. Wilson prosr.)
    vs)   T. A. B.
Charles Dyche)

               Continued by consent -
               Charles Dyche acknowl-
edged to owe the State of Tennessee one hundred Dollars
and Ironymus Dyche his Surety also acknowledged to owe
the State of Tennessee fifty dollars yet upon condition
that if Charles Dyche shall make his personal appearance
at the Court of pleas and quarter sessions to be held
for the county of Greene in the Court house in Greeneville on Wednesday next after the fourth Monday in July
next and stand his trial in this prosecution against
him and not depart the Court without leave then the above
recognizance to be void otherwise in force -

State of Tennessee

William Brannon prosr.)
    vs)   T. A. B.
Charles Nichols)

               This day came as well the
               Attorney General as the
Defendant in his proper person and the Defendant being

charged on the bill of Indictment for plea thereto says
that he is guilty in manner and form as charged in the
Bill of Indictment and puts himself on the mercy of the
Court. Therefore It is considered that the Defendant
for such his offence be fined forfeit and pay to the
State of Tennessee the Sum of one Dollar and that he pay
the Costs of this prosecution -

(P-46)
State of Tennessee
   vs
Henry Bailey cate issd

     Same
      vs vs Same
William Long

     Same
      vs vs same
Daniel Casteel

     Same
      vs vs same
William Jeens

     Same
      vs vs same
Benjamin Bowman

Polly Swatsel pauper   )
   vs   )   Case
William M. P. Mitchell)

         The proper Steps not having
         been taken in this Suit
It is ordered that the same be struck from the Docket.

Thomas Stroud   )
   vs   )   Certio
William Boling)

         On motion and Cause shewn by Af-
         fidavit of William Boling this
cause is continued until the next Term of this Court
until the next Term of this Court and set for trial on
Thursday of next Court by consent -

(P-47)
State of Tennessee
  and Thomas Harvey

vs)   Certio
John Thomason)

On motion of plaintiff by Attorney
a Rule is allowed to shew cause
why the defendants petition and Writ should be dismissed.

State of Tennessee)
William Strong prosr.)
vs)
Philip T. Babb.-)

On motion of the Defendant
by attorney and with the
Assent of the Court a Nolli prosequi is entered in this
prosecution - And thereupon came James McCollum and
Levi Babb and assumed for and on behalf of the Defendant the payment of the Costs of this prosecution and
agree that Judgment be entered against them for the
same - Therefore It is considered that the State of Tennessee recover against the said James McCollum and Levi
Babb the Costs aforesaid according to their assumpsit -

State of Tennessee

William Strong prosr.)
vs)
Philip T. Babb)

On motion of the Defendant
by Attorney and with the
assent of the Court a Nolli prosequi is entered in this
prosecution and thereupon came James McCollum and Levi
Babb and assumed for and on behalf of the Defendant the
payment of the Costs of this prosecution and agree that
Judgment be entered against them for the same -
Therefore It is considered that the State of Tennessee
(P-48) recover against the said James McCollum and
Levi Babb the Costs aforesaid according to their Assumpsit

State of Tennessee

Thomas Dodd prosr.)
vs)   Misdemeanor &c.
Philip Babb)

On motion and with the assent
of the Court a Nolli prosequi
is entered in this prosecution and thereupon came Peter
Dillon and assumed and undertook the payment of the Costs
and agrees that Judgment be entered against him for the
Same - Therefore It is considered that the State of

Tennessee recover against the said Peter Dillon the
costs of this prosecution according to his Assumpsit -

Thomas Harvey)
   vs) Certio
John Thomason)

       Continued by Consent

State of Tennessee)
   vs) Bastardy
Gross Scruggs)

           The Defendant who stands bound
           by recognizance in the Sum of
One hundred dollars for his Appearance here at the present
day to answer rhe State of Tennessee of a charge alledged
against him for begeting a Bastard child of the Body of
Edith Woods of this County single woman was solemnly
called for that purpose but came not and made default.
Therefore It is considered that the State of Tennessee recover   (P-49)   against the said Gross Scruggs the Sum
of One hundred Dollars the amount of his recognizance in
this behalf acknowledged unless sufficient cause for such
failure be shewn - And thereupon Hugh Maloney, Robert Mc-
Kemy and Alexander Sevier who stand bound by recognizance
in the Sum of one hundred dollars for the appearance here
at the present day of Gross Scruggs and answer the State
of Tennessee of a charge of Bastardy were severally solemnly called to bring into Court the Body of the said
Gross Scruggs and surrender the same in discharge of themselves as bail but failed so to do and made Default.
Therefore It is considered that the State of Tennessee
recover against the said Hugh Malony, Robert McKemy and
Alexander Sevier the aforesaid Sum of one hundred Dollars
the amount of their recognizance in this behalf acknowledged unless sufficient cause be shewn -

Phobe King (pauper))
   vs) Case
William Blair)

           The proper Steps not having
           been taken in this Suit it is
ordered that the same be struck from the Docket.

John Matthews, Assgne)
John Nooncaster)
   vs) Applt.
George Bell)

On motion Ordered that the plaintiff give Security
for the Costs of this Suit on or before Monday of next
Court or the same will be dismissed.

(P-50)
Henry Fearbe)
vs)   Certio
Moses G. Wilson)

The petition of the Defendant
was presented by James P. Taylor
esquire his attorney praying writs of Certiorari and Supersedeas - Upon Consideration whereof It is ordered that
said Petition be granted and that Writs issue pursuant
to the prayer of the same on bond and Security being
given according to law -

Peter Parsons)
vs)   Motion &c.
Arthur G. Armstrong and)
Amis Grantham)

It appearing in evidence
to the Court that the
plaintiff become Security for the Defendants in an appeal from the Judgment of the County to the Circuit
Court of Greene County that in consequence of becoming
Security as aforesaid he has been compelled to pay the
Sum of Forty five Dollars and ninety seven Cents - Therefore on motion of the said Peter Parsons by James P. Taylor his Attorney It is considered that he recover against
the said Arthur G. Armstrong and Amis Grantham the aforesaid Sum of forty five Dollars ninety Seven cents and the
Costs of this Motion -

(P-51)
John Kifer)
vs)   Original Attachment
The Estate of)
Thomas Davis)

On motion of the plaintiff and it
appearing to the Satisfaction of
the Court that Thomas Davis the Defendant is an Inhabi-
tant of North Carolina - It is therefore ordered that the
proceedings in this Cause be staid Six months and that
a Summons issue directing the Sheriff to Summon three
Justices to ascertain and certify whether the property
of the defendant levied on by the Constable be perishable or not and should the same be reported perishable
and not replevied within Sixty days - that the same be
sold according act of Assembly.

Thomas Dodd)
    vs)   Case for Words.
Julien Green)

               Thomas Bailey for himself
               and others appearance Bail
               of the Defendant in this suit
               produced and surrendered in
               open Court the body of said
               Defendant in discharge of
               themselves as Bail. Whereupon
               the said Defendant is charged
               in Custody of the Sheriff who
               being present in Court takes
               charge of him accordingly

     And thereupon the parties by Attorneys being present
came also a Jury to wit. William Trobaugh, Levi Dunn,
John Walker, William Likens, Jacob Garrett, John Lauderdale, Isaac Fox, Marmaduke Lamb   (P-52)   Jacob Rymal
Eli Rambo, Ironymus Dyche, and Emanuel Dyche who being
elected tried and sworn the truth to speak upon the Issues joined upon their Oath do say that the Defendant of
his own wrong and without any Such cause as in pleading
he hath alledged did speak and publish the defamatory
words in the Declaration mentioned that he was guilty
of speaking and publishing the same within six months
next before the issuance of the original Writ of the
plaintiff in this cause as the plaintiff by replying
hath alledged and that the Defendant was not justified
in speaking and publishing said Defamatory words as the
plaintiff by replying to the third and fourth pleas of
the Defendants hath alledged and they do assess the plaintiffs Damages by Occasion thereof to two Dollars –

     Therefore It is considered that the plaintiff recover
against the Defendant the Sum of Two dollars the Damages
by the Jury assessed and also the Sum of Two Dollars of
his Costs by him about his Suit in this behalf expended.

William Wilson)
    vs)   Debt. Demurrer to
Jane Russell Admr.)   amended plea
    of John Russell decd.)

               This day came the parties
               by attornies and thero-
upon the Demurrer to the amended plea came on for Argument
whereupon all and singular the premises being seen and by
the Court fully understood It is considered that said Demurrer be sustained. And thereupon came also a Jury towit
Joseph Bruner   (P-53)   Philip Bird, William Lawson,

Charles Nicholas, Amos McBride, Isaac Earnest, Thomas
Wilson, Samuel Standfield Daniel Britton, James McCollum, William Grubbs and William Mitchell who being elected tried and sworn the truth to speak upon the issues
joined upon the issues joined upon their Oath do say
that John Russell the Intestate of the said Defendant
did not in his lifetime pay the Debt in the Declaration as in pleading she hath alledged and they do assess the plaintiff damages by reason of the Detention
of the Debt in the Declaration mentioned to Two Thousand
Six hundred and Twenty four Dollars and forty Seven Cents
And the Jurors aforesaid upon their Oath aforesaid do
farther say that the Defendant Jane Russell hath fully
administered all and singular the Goods and Chattles
Rights and Credits which were of John Russell decd. that
had come to he hands to be administered at the time of
bringing this Suit Therefore It is concluded that the
Defendant Jane Russell go hence without day and that the
Plaintiff recover against the heirs of John Russell
decd. if they have real estate by Descent the Sum of
nine thousand three hundred and twenty eight dollars
and ninety four cents to be discharged by the lesser
Sum of four thousand five hundred and thirty eight Dollars with the Damages by the Jury aforesaid assessed
and the Costs - but before any execution shall issue on
said Judgment against said heirs a Scire Facias shall
issue calling on them to shew cause why the real estate
of John Russell which may devised or decended to them
shall not be sold to satisfy said Judgment and Costs -
And it being now suggested to the Court that Joseph
Cutler and Lorenda M. His Wife formerly   (P-54)
Lorinda M. Russell, Alfred Russell, Daniel M. Russell,
Thomas A. M. Russell on the children and heirs at ----
of John Russell decd. and it being suggested that the
three last mentioned heirs are Infants under the Age of
Twenty one years, And it appearing that the plaintiff has
endeavored to get a Guardian appointed and failed to suc-
ceed - It is therefore ordered that Joseph Cutler be appointed special Guardian Pendenti Leti to receive Scire
Facias and defend this Suit for and on behalf of said
heirs.

                    Grand Jurors
                    discharged 2 Days

And Court adjourned until tomorrow morning 9 Oclock

                              E. D. Hale
                              R. West
                              M. Lincoln J. P.

Thursday 27th April 1826

Court met present

The minutes of yesterdays proceedings were read
and signed -

Thos Dodd   )
    vs   )   Case for words
Julien Greene   )

                   The plaintiff releases the defendant
        (P-55)   from the Custody of the
Sheriff, on Condition that execution issue for the Damages
and Costs by him recovered which is ordered accordingly

John Balch   )
    vs   )   Certio.
James McPheran   )

                   On motion of Plaintiff by Attorney
    a Rule is allowed him to shew cause
why the Defendants Petition and Writ should be dismissed.

Samuel Walker   )
    vs   )   Appl.
Zachariah Kinnamon Applt.   )

                   The plaintiff at the pres-
ent Term of this Court
having been ordered to give Security for the Costs of this
Suit came John M. Kilgore and Charles Love and assumed for
and on behalf of the Plaintiff that if he shall be cast
in this Suit that he will pay the Costs or that the said
John M. Kilgore and Charles Love will do ti for him -

Joseph Allen   )
    vs   )   Debt Writ of inquiry
William L. French   )
Abraham Lain and   )
Thomas Loyd   )

                   This day came the parties by
Attornies and thereupon a Jury
to wit George Bell Jacob Garrett, Abraham Haines, Jeremiah
Casteel, Henry A. Farnsworth, William Mitchell, James Lowrey, Marmaduke Lamb, Zachariah Kinnamon, Peter Whittenberg
Weston McKahen, and John Walker who being elected tried
and sworn well and truly to enquire of Damages between the
parties upon their Oath do say that the (P-56) plaintiff has sustained Damages by reason of the Detention of
the Debt in the Declaration to Seventeen Dollars and Seventy five cents. And the Defendants in their proper persons

come and say that on the finding of the Jury in this Cause no Judgment ought to be rendered against them because they say Debt in the Debet & Detinet will not lie on the Note sued and because the Writ is in the Detinet & the Declaration in the Debet & Detinet - For these and other reasons to be seen in the Record they pray that Judgment be arrested

> Wm. L. French
> Abm. Lane
> Thos. Loid

Whereupon Argument of Counsel being heard and all and singular the premises being seen and by the Court fully understood - It is considered that the Reasons aforesaid in Arrest of Judgment be overruled and that the Plaintiff recover against the Defendants the Sum of one hundred five Dollars the Debt in the declaration mentioned except the Sum of Two Dollars eighty three Cents and 1.3 with the Damages by the Jury aforesaid assessed and his Costs by him about his suit in this behalf expended. From which Judgment the Defendants by attorney pray an appeal in the nature of a Writ of error to the next Circuit Court of Law to be held for the County of Greene in the Court house in Greeneville on the first Monday in September next and having given Bond and Security for the prosecution of their Appeal and having assigned Error - their Appeal is granted and the proceedings ordered to be certified

(P-57) During the progress of the above trial the Defendants by Attorney tender a Bill of exception to the Judgment of the Court &c. which is signed and sealed and ordered to be made a part of the Record.

William Brown	)	
vs	)	Certio
Isaac Jones	)	

This day came the parties by Attorneys and thereupon a Jury to wit Daniel Delany, James Marsh, Charles Hays, John Casteel, Jonathan Luster, Enos Williams, John Maltsberger George Kennedy, Thomas Oliphant, Isaac Earnest, Philip Bird and John Click who being elected tried and sworn well and truly to try this cause upon their oath do say that they find for the Plaintiff Twelve Dollars and fifty Cents - Therefore it is considered that the plaintiff

recover against the defendant and Michael Bright security
for the prosecution of his writ of Certiorari the Sum of
Twelve Dollars and fifty Cents and his Costs by him
about his suit in this behalf expended -

Stephen Huff and Joseph Huff)
  executors of John Huff Decd.)
   vs   )   Covenant
John Wealty Defendant   )

           This day came the
           parties by Attornies
and thereupon a Jury to wit George Welty Martin Fry,
Isaac Bible, Henry Fearle, James Smith Edward Casteel,
Charles Love, David Key, John Hoy, Reubin Dotson, Robert
Hays, Isaac Harmon, who being elected tried and sworn
the truth to speak upon the issue joined upon their Oath
do say that the Defendant hath not kept and performed
his Covenant as in pleading he hath (P-58) alledged
but hath broken the same in manner and form as the plaintiff
against him in his Declaration hath complained and they do
assess the plaintiffs Damages by occasion thereof to Two
hundred and Twenty eight Dollars - Therefore It is considered that the plaintiff recover against the Defendant the
Damages by the Jury assessed and his Costs by him about
his Suit in this behalf -

Stephen Huff and Joseph Huff   )
  executors of John Huff decd.)
   vs   ) Covenant
John Wealty Defendant   )

           This day came the
           parties by Attor-
nies and thereupon a Jury to wit George Welty, Martin
Fry, Isaac Bible, Henry Fearle, James Smith, Edward Casteel, Charles Love, David Key, John Hoy, Reubin Dotson,
Robert Hays, and Isaac Harmon who being elected tried and
sworn the truth to speak upon the issue joined upon their
Oath do say that the defendant hath not kept and performed
his Covenabt as in pleading he hath alledged but hath
broken the same in manner and form as the plaintiff against
him in his declaration hath complained and they do assess
the plaintiffs Damages by occasion thereof to two hundred
and Twenty eight Dollars - Therefore It is considered that
the plaintiff recover against the Defendant the Damages
aforesaid by the Jury assessed and his costs by him about
his Suit in this behalf expended -

Stephen Huff and Joseph Huff)
  executor of John Huff decd.)
   vs   ) Cont.
John Wealty   )

This day came the parties by Attornies   (P-59)
and therefore a Jury to wit George Welty Martin Fry,
Isaac Bible, Henry Fearle, James Smith, Edward Casteel
Charles Love David Key, John Hoy, Reubin Dotson, Robert
Hays, and Isaac Harmon who being elected tried and sworn
the truth to speak upon the issue joined upon their Oath
do say that the Defendant hath not kept and performed his
Covenant as in pleading he hath alledged but hath broken
the same in manner and form as the plaintiff against him
in his declaration hath complained and they do assess
the plaintiffs Damages by occasion thereof to Two hundred
and fifty Dollars – Therefore It is considered that the
plaintiff recover against the Defendant the Damages
aforesaid by the Jury aforesaid assessed and their Costs
by them about their Suit in this behalf expended.

Thomas Batt)
    vs   )   Sci Fa.
James Sevier)

This day came the parties by attornies
and thereupon a Jury to wit   George
Welty, Martin Fry, Isaac Bible, Henry Fearle, James Smith,
Edward Casteel, Charles Love, David Key, John Hoy, Reubin
Dotson, Robert Hays and Isaac Harmon who being elected
tried and sworn the truth to speak upon the issue joined
upon their Oath do say that the Defendant has not paid the
Costs in the Writ of Scire Facias named The plaintiff by
Attorney admiting the payment of the Debt in the Writ aforesaid named – Therefore It is considered that the Plaintiff
may have execution against the defendant for the Sum of
Twenty Six Dollars Seventy Two and One half Cents the Costs
in the Writ of Scire Facias named and that the plaintiff
recover against the Defendant his Costs expended in suing
forth and prosecuting his Writ of Scire Facias

(P-60)
James W. Paxton)
    vs   )   Debt
Daniel M. Guin)

This day came the parties by
attorneys and thereupon a Jury
towit   George Welty, Martin Fry, Isaac Bible, Henry Farle,
James Smith, Edward Casteel, Charles Love, David Key, John
Hoy, Reubin Dotson, Robert Hays and Isaac Harmon who being
elected tried and sworn the Truth to speak upon the issue
joined upon their oath do say that the Defendant has not
paid the Debt in the declaration mentioned as in pleading
he hath alledged and they do assess the plaintiffs Damages
by occasion thereof to Twenty four Dollars and eighty Cents
Therefore It is considered that the plaintiff recover against
the Defendant the Sum of One hundred and Twenty Dollars with
the Damages by the Jury aforesaid assessed and his Costs by
him about his Suit in this behalf expended

Scott Terry Administrator)
   of Hercules Scott decd.)
      vs)   Debt
Robert Brabson)

        . This day came the parties by attornies and thereupon a Jury to wit George Welty, Martin Fry, Isaac Bible, Henry Fearle, James Smith, Edward Casteel, Charles Love, David Key, John Hoy, Reubin Dotson, Robert Harp, and Isaac Harmon who being elected tried and sworn well and truly to try this cause upon their oath do say that the Defendant has not paid the Debt in the Declaration mentioned to the plaintiffs Intestate as the plaintiff by replying to the first plea of the Defendant hath alledged - And the Jurors aforesaid   (P-61)   upon their Oath aforesaid do farther say that the defendant did not pay the Debt in the Declaration mentioned to Scott Terry Administrator of Hercules Scott before the issuance of the original in this Cause as the plaintiff by replying to the second plea of the Defendant hath alledged and they do assess the plaintiffs Damages by reason of the Detention of the Debt in the Declaration mentioned to forty eight dollars and forty seven Cents - Therefore It is considered that the plaintiff recover against the Defendant the sum of Sixty five Dollars the Debt in the Declaration mentioned with the Damages by the Jury aforesaid assessed and his costs by him about his Suit in this behalf expended -

John Gass for Odells)
   and Blanton use)
      vs)   Debt
Alexander Sevier)

        This day came the parties by attornies and thereupon a Jury towit Daniel Delany, James Marsh, Charles Hays, John Casteel, Jonathan Lintz, Enos Williams, John Maltsberger, George Kennedy, Thomas Oliphant, Isaac Earnest, Philip Bird and Samuel Standfield who being elected tried and sworn the truth to speak upon the issue joined upon their Oath do say that the defendant has not paid the Debt in the declaration mentioned and they do assess the plaintiffs Damages by occasion thereof to fifteen Dollars and ninety three Cents - Therefore it is considered that the plaintiff recover against the defendant the Sum of One hundred One Dollars and twenty cents the Debt in the declaration mentioned with the Damages by the Jury assessed and his costs by him about his Suit in this behalf expanded.

(P-62)
Martin Fry)
      vs)   Applt.
Vincent Fry Applt.)

The plaintiff having been ordered to give Security
for the Costs of this Suit came Samuel Walker and assumed for the plaintiff that if he shall be cast in
this Suit that he will pay the Costs or that he the
said Samuel Walker will do it for him.

And thereupon came a Jury to wit George Bell, Jacob
Garrett, Abraham Hains, Jeremiah Casteel, Henry A. Farnsworth, William Mitchell, James Lowrey, Peter Whittenberg,
Weston McKeehan, William Brown, Isaac Bible, and Henry
Fearle, who being elected tried and sworn well and truly
to try this cause upon their oath do say that they find
for the plaintiff eight Dollars.

> And on motion of Defendant
> by Attorney a Rule is allowed
> him to shew cause why a new
> trial should be granted —
> Whereupon all and singular
> the premises being seen and
> by the Court fully understood
> It is considered that said
> Rule be made absolute —

Marmaduke Lamb   )
        vs   )   Appl.
Charles Love Applt.   )

On motion and Cause shewn by
Affidavit of Defendant this
Cause is continued until next Court.

(P-63)
James Hise   )
        vs   )   Debt
Allen Gillespie and   )
Isaac Wilson   )

This day came the parties by
attornies and thereupon a
Jury to wit   Daniel Delany, James Marsh, Charles Hays,
John Casteel, Jonathan Lints, Enos Williams, John Maltsberger, George Kennedy, Thomas Oliphant, Isaac Earnest,
Philip Bird and Samuel Standfield who being elected
tried and sworn the truth to speak upon the issue joined
upon their oath do say that the Defendants have not paid
the Debt in the Declaration mentioned as in pleading they
have alledged and they do assess the plaintiff's Damages
by occasion thereof to fifteen dollars and ninety three
cents Therefore it is considered that the plaintiff recover against the Defendants the sum of One hundred and
fifty Dollars the Debt in the declaration mentioned with

the Damages aforesaid by the Jury aforesaid assessed and
his costs by him about his Suit in this behalf expended

George Bell   )
       vs   )   Certio
Henry A. Farnsworth   )

This day came the parties by
Attorneys and thereupon a
Jury to Wit   Daniel Delany, James Marsh, Charles Hays
John Casteel, Jonathan Lints, Enos Williams, John Malts-
berger, George Kennedy, Thomas Oliphant, Isaac Earnesr,
Philip Bird, Samuel Standfield, who being elected tried and
Sworn well and truly to try this Cause upon their Oath
do say that they find for the plaintiff eight Dollars -

And on motion of Defendant
by Attorney a Rule is allowed
him to shew cause   (P-64)
why a new trial should be
granted Whereupon all and
singular the premises being
seen and by the Court fully
understood It is considered
that said Rule be made absolute

State of Tennessee   )
       vs   )   T. A. B. on Philip Bird
Howell Houston   )

On motion and cause shewn
by affidavit of Defendant
this prosecution is continued untill the next term of
this Court - Howell Houston acknowledged to owe the
State of Tennessee the Sum of one hundred Dollars yet
upon condition that if Howell Houston shall make his
personal appearance at the Court of pleas and Quarter
Sessions to be held for the County of Greene in the
Court house in Greeneville on Wednesday next after the
fourth Monday in July next and stand his trial in this
prosecution against him and not depart the Court without
leave then the above recognisance to be void otherwise
in force -

John Miller   )
       vs   )
James R. Isbell and   )
Mordecai Lincoln   )

This day came the plaintiff
by Attorney and the Defendants

not appearing says nothing in Bar of the Scire Facias
of the plaintiff whereby the plaintiff remains against
the said Defendants therein undefended - Therefore It is
considered that the plaintiff may have execution against
the Defendants for the Sum of One hundred fifty One Dollars fifty three Cents the debt in the Writ of Scire
Facias named with interest thereon from the 25th day of
January 1855   (P-65)   and also the Sum of nine Dollars and fifty four cents for Costs and that the plaintiff recover against the Defendants his costs expended
in sueing forth and prosecuting his Writ of Scire Facias.

Barbara Kirk   )
    for herself and as   )
    Guardian of the minor   )
    heirs of Joseph Kirk decd.   )
)
)
    vs   )   petition &c.
)
Joseph Davis   )

                                      Replication filed
                                      and set for hear-
                                      ing by Complainants
                                      Counsel.

Daniel Delany   )
    vs   )   Certio
Joseph Powell   )

                     This day came the parties by attor-
                     neys and thereupon a Jury to wit
George Welty, Martin Fry, Isaac Bible, Henry Fearle, James
Smith, Edward Casteel, Charles Love, David Key, John Hoy,
Reubin Dotson, Robert Hays and Isaac Harmon who being
elected tried and sworn well and truly to try this cause
upon their oath do say that they find for the plaintiff
Two Dollars - Therefore It is considered that the plain-
tiff recover against the Defendant and William Hull (of
Alexander security for the prosecution of his writ of Certiorari the aforesaid Sum of Two Dollars and his costs
by him about his Suit in this behalf expended - From which
Judgment the Defendant by Attorney prays an Appeal to the
next Circuit Court of law to be held for the County of
Greene in the Court house in Greeneville on the first
Monday in September next and having given Bond and Security to prosecute in his Appeal is granted and the proceedings ordered to be certified -

(P-66)
Samuel Dunwoody   )
    vs   )   Debt
Jacob Dyche   )

The Defendant by attorney withdraws the Demurrer in this Cause and confessed Judgment according to Specialty - Therefore It is considered that the plaintiff recover against the defendant the Sum of three hundred dollars the amount of the Specialty declared on with the further Sum of Nineteen Dollars eighty Seven and one half Cents for Interest due and accrued on the same and his Costs by him about his Suit in this behalf expended.

Same)
   vs)   Debt
Same)

     The Defendant by Attorney withdraws the Demurrer in this Cause and confesses Judgment according to specialty - therefore It is considered that the plaintiff recover against the Defendant the Sum of three hundred Dollars the amount of the specialty declared on with the further Sum of thirty Seven Dollars eighty Seven and one half Cents for Interest due and accrued in the same and his costs by him about his Suit in this behalf expended

Same)   Debt
   vs)
Same)

     The Defendant by Attorney withdraws the Demurrer in this Cause and confesses Judgment according to Specialty - Therefore It is considered that the plaintiff recover against the Defendant the Sum of Two hundred and eight dollars   (P-67) and fifty nine Cents the Residue of the Debt and Interest on the Specialty declared on and his costs by him about his Suit in this behalf expended.

Samuel Walker)
   vs)   Appl.
Zachariah Kinnamon)
     Applt)

     This day came the parties by Attornies and thereupon a Jury to Wit Daniel Delany, James Smith, Samuel Standfield James Marsh, John Hoy, Reubin Dotson, John Casteel, Garrett Dillon, Charles Nichols, Samuel White, Henry A. Farnsworth and Daniel Olinger, who being elected tried and sworn well and truly to try this Cause upon their Oath do say that they find the plaintiff Nine Dollars sixty Two and One half Cents. Therefore It is considered that the plaintiff recover against the Defendant and Daniel Borden security for the prosecution of his Appeal the aforesaid Sum of nine Dollars

Sixty two and One half Cents and his Costs by him about
his Suit in this behalf expended.

From which Judgment the
Defendant by Attorney

prays an Appeal in the nature of a Writ of Error to the
Nature of a Writ of Error to the next Circuit Court of
Law to be held for the County of Greene in the Court house
in Greeneville on the first Monday in September next and
having given bond and Security to prosecute - his Appeal
is granted and the proceedings Ordered to be certified -
errors Assigned

During the progress of this
Suit the Defendant by Attorney tenders his Bill of exceptions to the Judgment of
the Court &c. which is signed
and Sealed and ordered to be
made a part of the Record -

(P-68)
James H. Davis   )
    vs   )   Order Sale
George Jennings   )

Daniel McLane a Constable of Greene
County returned here into Court
an execution issued by George Wells esquire an acting Justice of the peace for said County against the estate of
the Defendant for the Sum of nineteen dollars and Twenty-
five Cents Debt and fifty Cents cost recovered by the
plaintiff against the Defendant before said Justice on the
13th day of August 1825 on which execution said Constable
has made return that he had levied on a certain tract of
land containing seventy Two Acres joining the land of John
Morgan, Hezekiah Danley and the heirs of Philip Maltsberger
decd. on Middle Creek - Therefore one motion of the plaintiff by - his Attorney It is considered that all the right
Title, interest claim and Demand of the said George Jennings
of in and to the aforesaid tract of and be condemned to the
satisfaction of the Recovery aforesaid and that the same
or so much thereof as well satisfy said Recovery and the
costs of this motion be sold as the law directs -

And Court adjourned
untill tomorrow morning
9 0 Clock

H. D. Hale
Joseph Davis
Cornelius Smith

Court met present

The minutes of yesterdays proceedings were read and signed

John Stephens   )
     vs   )   Debt
Joseph Rice   )

This day came the parties by attornies and thereupon a Jury towit   Thomas Dodd, William Mitchell, Daniel Olinger, Robert Hays, Martin Fry, Henry A Farnsworth, James Gass, James Jones, David Keller, Levi Dunn, Daniel Guin, and George McLain who being elected tried and sworn the truth to speak upon the issue joined upon their oath do say that the Defendant has paid the Debt in the declaration mentioned except the Sum of three hundred twenty nine Dollars and thirty seven cents and they do assess the plaintiffs Damages by occasion thereof to One Cent. Therefore It is considered that the plaintiff recover against the Defendant the Sum of three hundred Twenty nine Dollars and thirty Seven cents the Residue of the Debt in the Declaration mentioned with the Damages by the Jury aforesaid assessed and his Costs by him about his Suit in this behalf expended -

Charles W. Conway   )
     vs   )   Cont.
John A. Aiken   )

This day came the parties by attornies   (P-70)   and thereupon a Jury to wit Thomas Dodd, William Mitchell, Daniel Olinger, Robert Hays, Martin Fry, Henry A. Farnsworth, James Gass, James Jones, David Keller, Levi Dunn, Daniel Guin, and George McLain who being elected tried and sworn the truth to speak upon the issue joined upon their oath do say that the Defendant has not kept and performed his covenant as in pleading he hath alledged but hath broken the same in manner and form as the plaintiff against him in his declaration hath complained and they do assess the plaintiffs damages by occasion thereof to Seventy four dollars and fifty Cents. Therefore It is considered that the plaintiff recover against the Defendant the Damages by the Jury aforesaid assessed and his costs by him about his Suit in this behalf expended -

Frederick Trobaugh)
     vs   )   Debt
Jacob Dyche   )

This day came the parties by attornies and thereupon
a Jury to wit Thomas Dodd, William Mitchell, Daniel Olinger, Robert Hays, Martin Fry, Henry A. Farnsworth, James
Cass, James Jones, David Keller, Levi Dunn, Daniel Cuin,
and George McClain who being elected tried and sworn the
truth to speak upon the issue joined upon their oath do
say the Defendant has not paid the Debt in the Declaration
mentioned as in pleading he hath alledged and they do
asess the plaintiffs Damages by Occasion thereof to nine
Dollars and forty one cents - Therefore it is considered
the plaintiff recover against the Defendant the sum of
one hundred and fifty Dollars and seventy five cents the
Debt in the Declaration mentioned (P-71) with the Damages
by the Jury assessed and his costs by him about his suit
in this behalf expended -

Rachel Caldwell)
    vs   ) Case.
James McCroskey)

         Ordered by the Court that the cause be
struck from the Docket and that the costs of the same be
paid by the plaintiff.

Boyd McNairy   )
    vs.   ) Debt
Alexander Sevier)

         On motion and cause shewn by Affidavit
of Defendant this cause is continued untill the next Term
of this Court -

William Dickson   )
    vs   ) Case. Writ of Enquiry
John M. Kilgore, Administrator)
James Kilgore   )

         This day came the parties
by Attorneys and thereupon a jury to wit Thomas Lee, Jacob
Newman, John Brothertin, James Smith, John Myers, Ephraim
Dell, James McKeehan, Howell Houston, Samuel Walker, Abraham Haynes, William Brown and John Ross who being elected
tried and sworn well and truly to enquire of Damages between
the parties upon their oath do say that the plaintiff has
sustained Damages by occasion in the Declaration mentioned
to one hundred thirty nine dollars and sixty nine cents -
Therefore it is considered that the plaintiff recover against
the Defendant the aforesaid Sum of one hundredthirty nine
Dollars and sixty nine cents the Damages by the jury assessed
and his costs by him about his suit in this behalf expended

(P-72)
William Dickson)
    vs   ) Debt
Obadiah Neel   )

         This day came the parties by Attornies
and thereupon a jury to wit Thomas Dodd, William Mitchell,

Daniel Olinger, Robert Hays, Martin Fry, Henry A . Farnsworth, James Gass, David Keller, Levi Dunn, Daniel Guin, and George McLain, who being elected tried and sworn the truth to speak upon the issue joined upon their oath do say that the Defendant has paid the Debt in the Declaration mentioned except the sum of one hundred and Twenty Six Dollars and they do assess the plaintiffs Damages by occasion of the Detention of said Debt to Three cents - Therefore it is considered that the plaintiff recover against the Defendant the sum of one hundred and twenty six dollars the residue of the debt in the declaration mentioned with the Damages by the jury assessed and his costs by him about his suit in this behalf expended -

Valentine Sevier surviving)
partner of Deaderick & Sevier)
for the use of William H. Deaderick)
    vs)   Debt
Samuel Leming)

    This day came the parties by Attornies and thereupon a jury to wit, Reubin Dotson, Robert Smith, Edward Murphy, Peter Mismer, Joseph Powell, Wm. Engledow, Jacob Smelser, Jacob Dyche, Reubin West, James Kirk Benjamin Keller,and Samuel Bridewell, who being elected tried and sworn the truth to speak upon . (P-73) the issue joined upon their oath do say that the defendant has paid the Debt in the Declaration mentioned except the Sum of Two Hundred and six dollars and they do assess the plaintiffs Damages by occasion thereof to one cent - Therefore it is considered that the plaintiff recover against the Defendant the aforesaid sum of Two hundred Six Dollars the residue of the Debt in the Declaration mentioned with the Damages by the jury assessed and his costs by him about his suit in this behalf expended --

William Dickson)
    vs) Debt
John Love)

    This day came the parties by attornies and thereupon a jury to wit Reubin Dotson, Robert Smith, Edward Murphy, Teter Masoner, Joseph Powell, William Engledow, Jacob Smelser, Jacob Dyche,Reubin West, James Kirk, Benjamin Keller and Lemuel Bridewell who being elected tried and sworn the truth to speak upon joined upon their oath do say that the Defendant has not paid the Debt in the declaration mentioned and they do assess the plaintiffs damages by occasion thereof to thirty eight dollars and twenty six cents - Therefore it is considered that the plaintiff recover against the defendant the sum of Two hundred eight dollars nineteen and one half cents the debt in the Declaration mentioned with the damages by the jury assessed and his costs by him about his suit in this behalf expended -

Jacob T. Wyrick)
    vs   )   Certio
Andrew Park)

          Continued by consent.

James Smith & Wife)
    vs   )   Issue &c made up
Dunns Executors)

          By consent of the parties by attornies
this cause is transfered to the Circuit Court of Greene
County there to be tried and the clerk of this court is
directed to make out an extract and Bill of costs of this
Suit -

William McDannel)
     vs   )   Debt
Jacob Newman)

          On motion and cause shewn by affidavit
of Defendant this cause is continued untill next court

William Ballard Assignee)
David C. Posey)
    vs   )   Cont. Demurrer to Declaration
Hiram Hogan)

          This day came the parties by
Attorney and thereupon the Defendants Demurrer to Plaintiffs
Declaration came on for argument- Whereupon all and singular the premises being seen and by the court fully understood
It is considered that said Demurrer be overuled and that the
plaintiff recover against the defendant the Damages by occasion in the Declaration mentioned- But because it is unknown
to the Court what those Damages are- It is ordered that a
jury come here at the next Term of this Court to enquire of
Damages between the parties in this Suit -

(P-75)
Robert Dickson administrator)
of P.O. Collayhan Decd.)
    vs   )   Case
John Reah)

          This day came the Defendant
by Attorney and the plaintiff although solemnly called came
not neither is his suit prosecuted - Therefore it is considered that the plaintiff be Non Pros and that the defendant
recover against the plaintiff his costs by him about his
Defence in this behalf expended.

Peter Parsons)
    VS   )   Case in Assumpsit
Robert Dickson, Administrator)
of Patrick O. Callayhan decd.)

This day came the parties by Attornies and thereupon
a Jury to wit Thomas Dodd, William Mitchell, Daniel Olinger, Robert Hays, Martin Fry, Henry A. Farnsworth, James
Gass, James Jones, Daniel Keller, Levi Dunn, Daniel Guin,
and George McClain who being elected tried and sworn the
truth to speak upon the issues joined upon their oath do
say that that the Defendant did assume in manner and form
as the plaintiff by replying to the first plea of Defendant
hath alledged - that the Defendants Intestate did assume
as the plaintiff by replying to the Second plea of Defendant
hath alledged- that the Defendant did assume within three
years next- before the issuance of the original writ in this
cause - and that the Defendant hath not fully administered
all and singular the goods and chattels of his Intestate
that have come to his hands to be administered and they do
assess the plaintiffs damages by occasion thereof to one
hundred and twenty dollars- Therefore it is (P-76) considered that the plaintiff recover againstthe Defendant the
Damages by the jury aforesaid assessed to be levied of the
good and chattels of the Intestate when assets shall come
to the Defendants hand to be administered and also his costs-

Henry Rippetoe   )
  vs   )Appl.
Martin Fry Applt)This day came the parties by Attornies and
                  thereupon a jury to wit Reubin Dotson,
Robert Smith, Edward Murphy, Teter Masoner, Joseph Powell,
William Engledow, Jacob Smelser, Jacob Dyche, Reubin West,
James Kirk, Benjamin Keller, and Lemuel Bridewell who being
elected tried and sworn well and truly to try this cause
upon their oath do say that they find for the Defendant -
Therefore it is considered that the plaintiff take nothing
by his suit and that the Defendant recover against the
plaintiff his costs by him about his Defence in this behalf
expended -

Isaac Baker   )
  vs   ) Certio. Rule to Dismiss
Jacob Rymall) This day came the parties by attornies and
              thereupon the Rule entered to shew cause
why the Defendants petition and writ should be dismissed
came on for argument - Whereupon all and singular the premises being seen and by the Court fully understood - It is
considered that said Rule be discharged -

(P-77)
State of Tennessee)
  VS   ) Bastardy
James McKeehan   ) James McKeehan acknowledged to owe the
                   State of Tennessee one hundred Dollars
and Alfred Hunter and Richard M. Woods his Sureties also
acknowledged to owe the State of Tennessee the sum of one
hundred dollars each yet upon condition that if James Mc
Keehan shall make his personal appearance at the court of
pleas and quarter sessions to be held for the County of Greene

in the Court House in Greeneville on Wednesday next after
the fourth Monday in July next and answer the State of Tennessee of a charge alledged against him for begeting a Bastard
child of the body of Polly Swatsel of this County single
woman and not depart the Court without leave then the above
recognizance to be void otherwise in force -

The last Will and Testament of Jacob Linebough Senr. was
produced in court for probat by Jacob Linebough and Jacob
Linebough (of John) the executors named in said Will - and
thereupon Benjamin Keller and Rosanna his wife and David
Keller and Mary his wife came into court in their proper persons and oppose the probat of said Will and pray that an issue
may be made up to try whether the paper purporting to be the
last will and testament of Jacob Linebough Senr. is his last
will and testament or not -

Whereupon it is ordered that an issue be made up and that
a jury come here at the next Term of this court to try whether
the paper purporting to be the last will and testament of the
said Jacob Linebough Senr. is the true last will will and
Testament of the said Jacob Linebough or not -

Abraham Tucker   )
and Mary Ann his wife, Compts, Pltff. &c.) This cause coming
    vs.   ) on to be heard on
Jacob Newman and John Hardin, executors   ) the petition of Complainants answer of
of the last Will & Testament of   ) plainants answer of
Cornelius Newman, Decd.   ) respondents replication and proof and
                                            it appearing to the

Satisfaction of the Court that the said Cornelius Newman & Rebecca Britton administered on the personal estate of John Britton
decd. at the January Session of the Court in the year 1805.
that said administrator and administratrix sold the personal
estate amounting to $350.47 and returned an account Sales to
July Session 1805 that there were eight distributees of said
estate including the widow who were each entitled to $30.00
with interest thereon from 22nd. July 1807 at the rate of Six
Pr Centum Pr Annum which Interest amounts to the sum of $30
amounting in all to the Sum $60. out of which Sum the Court
allow the Sum of Seven Dollars being one eighth part of the
funeral expenses and charges due said administrator and administratrix - Whereupon it is ordered adjudged and decrad that
the plaintiffs recover of said Newman and Hardin executors of
Cornelius Newman decd. the sum of sixty dollars the amount of
their share of said personal estate to be levied of the goods
and chattels of said Cornelius Newman decd. in their hands to
be administered and the costs of this suit for which execution
may issue

                                    John Mauris
                                    Wm. McBride
                                    John Gass, Jr.

(P-79)   From which judgment and decree the Defendants by
Attorney and pray an Appeal to the next Circuit Court to be
held for the County of Greene in the Court House in Greeneville on the first Monday in September next and having given
Bond and security to prosecute - their Appeal is granted and
the proceedings ordered to be certified -

    During the progress of this Suit the Defendants by Attor-
ney tender a Bill of exceptions to the judgment of the
Court &c. which is signed and sealed and ordered to be
made a part of the Record. -

George McClain)
   vs   )   Motion for Judgment for surplus monies
John Brothertin)   made on executions against plaintiff
                and not paid over -

    This day came the parties by Attornies and thereupon the
plaintiffs motion heretofore entered came on for argument -
Whereupon all and singular the premises being seen and by
the Court fully understood - It is considered that motion
be overruled and that the Defendant recover against the plaintiff the costs of this motion -

George Manes   )
  vs.   )   Motion for judgment for failing to make
Ellet Rutherford)   ..and pay over monies on execution the
                plaintiff against Reubin West -

    This day came the parties by Attornies and thereupon the
plaintiffs motion heretofore entered came on for argument.
Whereupon all and singular the premises being seen and by
the Court fully understood (P-80)   It is considered that
said motion be overruled and that the Defendant recover
against the Plaintiff the costs of this motion -

John Balch   )
   vs   ) Certio. Rule to dismiss
James McPherran   )

          The Plaintiff by Attorney discharges the
Rule heretofore entered to dismiss the defendants petition
and writ --

Jacob Smiles   )
   VS   )   Debt
William M. P. Mitchell)
and Moses G. Wilson   )   The plaintiff by his Attorney,
                Aaron Finch dismisses his Suit
and assumes the cost. Therefore it is considered that the
Defendants recover against the plaintiff their costs by them
about their suit in this behalf expended. -

Benjamin Keller and Rosanna   )
his wife and David Keller   )   Issue made up &c.
and Mary his wife   )
    vs   )   On motion and cause shewn
Jacob Linebough and Jacob   )   by affidavit of Jacob Line-
Linebough of John executors   )   bough a commission is award-
of Jacob Linebough Senr.   )   ed the Defendants to take
                      the deposition of Samuel B.

Hawkins, which may be directed to anyone justice of the peace for Greene County by giving the plaintiffs five days notice of the time and place of executingsuch commission.

Pettit Jurors discharged 4 days.

(P-81)

Boyd McNairy)
vs) Debt
Alexander Sevier)

On motion and cause shewn by affidavit of Defendant a commission is awarded him to take take the Deposition on Stockley Hays of Madison County which may be directed to any one Justice of the Peace for said County by giving the plaintiff ten days notice of the time and place of executing such commission -

Robert Dickson, Administrator)
of Patrick O Callayhan Decd.) Case
vs) This day came the parties
William K. Vance) by Attornies and thereupon
a jury to wit Reubin Dotson
Robert Smith, Edward Murphey, Teter Masoner, Joseph Powell, William Engledow, Jacob Smelser, Jacob Dyche, Reubin West, James Kirk, Benjamin Keller, and Lemuel Bridewell who being elected tried and sworn the truth to speak upon the issues joined upon their oath do say that the Defendant did assume in manner and form as the Plaintiff against him in his declaration hath complained that he did assume within three years next before the issuance of the original writ in this cause as the plaintiff by reply ining to the second plea of the Defendant hath alledged - And the Jurors aforesaid upon their oath do say that the Defendant is entitled to a Set off against the claim of the plaintiff of $441.57½ for the amount of a judgment obtained in the Court of Pleas and Quarter Sessions of Greene County (P-82) against the plaintiff Intestate with interest thereon from 30th. July 1823 and also the further sum of $55.74 the amount of judgment obtained before Joseph Brown esquire against said intestate also the further sum of $22.31¼ cents for an account of tavern expenses and accounts paid to Guin and Garvin for said Intestate as is set forth in his notice of set off leaving a balance of $51.12 3/4 due the plaintiff and the jurors aforesaid upon their oath a foresaid do further say that the defendant did not tender to the plaintiff the sum of $51.12 3/4 before the issuance of the original writ in this cause but that he brought the same into court at the return thereof as in pleading he hath alledged and they do assess the plaintiffs Damages by occasion thereof to fifty one dollars twelve and three fourth cents -

Therefore it is considered that the plaintiff recover against the Defendant the Damages by the jury aforesaid assessed and also the costs of the writ issued in this cause and the costs of the execution thereof and that the Defendant recover against the plaintiff the residue of the costs in this behalf expended -

And Court adjourned untill tomorrow morning 9 O'clock -

Richard West
Leo Stoner

(P-83)
        Court met present

The minutes of this days proceedings being read Court adjourned untill Court in course untill which time all matters and things in the same depending and undetermined are continued -

(P-84)
State of Tennessee

Be it remembered that at a Court of Pleas and Quarter Sessions continued and held for the County of Greene in the Courthouse in Greeneville on the fourth Monday being the 24th day of July 1826.
        was present.

Henry Pearle   )
    VS   )   Certio
Moses G. Wilson   )
                        The petition of the Defendant having been filed at the last Term of this Court praying Writs of Certiorari and Supersedeas and Writs not having issued. It is now ordered that Writs issue pursuant to the prayer of said petition on Bond and Security being given according to law.

John Matthews, Assignee)
John Nooncaster   )   Appl.
    VS   )
George Bell,Applt.   ) The plaintiff having been ordered
                            to give Security for the costs of this Suit came Ira Greene and assumed for and on behalf of the said plaintiff that if he shall be cast in this Suit that he will pay the costs or that he the said Ira Guin will do it for him.

(P-85)
Benjamin Keller and wife &)
David Keller and wife   )   Issue to try the last Will
    VS   )   and Testament of Jacob Line-
Jacob Linebough exr.   )   bough decd.
of Jacob Linebough decd.   )
                            The Plaintiff by their Attorney dismiss their Suit and assume the payment of the costs. Therefore it is considered that the Defendant recover against the plaintiffs his costs by him about Suit in this behalf expended -

Hannah Baker)
    VS   )   Certio
Isaac Baker   )
                    The petition of the Defendant was present by James P. Taylor esquire his Attorney praying Writs of Certiorari and Supersedeas upon Consideration whereof. It is ordered that Writs issue pursuant to the prayer of said petition on

bond and security being given according to Law

Robert Landrum)
  VS   )   Ca Sa issued by a Justice of the Peace.
Gross Scruggs)

        The Defendant having been arrested by Virtue of a Ca. Sa. and now appearing and having taken the Benefit of the Insolvent Debtors Oath. It is ordered that he be discharged and that the plaintiff pay the costs in this behalf expended.

Isaac Jester)
  VS   )   Ca. Sa. issued by a Justice of the Peace.
John Kesterson)
     Junior) The Defendant having been (P-86) arrested
           by virtue of a Ca. Sa. and now appearing and having taken the Benefit of the Insolvent debtors oath. It is ordered that he be discharged and that the plaintiff pay the costs in this behalf expended -
        And Court adjourned untill tomorrow morning 9 O'clock.

        Tuesday 25th. July 1826.
        Court met present.

        The Minutes of Yesterdays proceedings were read and signed -

Valentine Sevier, surviving partner)
of Deaderick & Sevier, Assignee &c.)   Covenant
for the use of Jos. Deaderick   )
     VS.   )   The Writ issued in this
Joseph Rutherford and   )   cause having been return-
James Rutherford   )   ed that the Defendants
                      were not found - On
motion of the plaintiff by James P. Taylor a judicial attachment is awarded him against the estate of the Defendants returnable here at next Court -

(P-87)
Marmaduke Lamb   )
   vs   )   Appl.
Charles Love, Applt.)

        This day came the parties by Attornies and thereupon a jury to wit, Jeremiah Farnsworth, Wyatt Hill, Absolom Thompson, James Goodin, Marmaduke McNeese, Samuel Mitchell, Henry A. Farnsworth, William McAmish, John Britton, John McAmish, John McKahan and Robert Simpson who being elected tried and sworn well and truly to try - this cause upon their oath do say that they find for the plaintiff one dollar and seventy five cents. Therefore it is considered by the Court that the plaintiff recover against the Defendant and George A. Starnes security for the prosecution of his appeal the aforesaid sum of one dollar and seventy five cents with interest thereon at the Rate of 12¼ pr cent thereon from the 17th. day of May 1825 and his costs by him about his suit in this behalf expended -

(P-88)

Johnson Frazier for the	)
use of Thomas Frasier	) Certio.
vs	)
Isaac Walker	) On motion of Defendant by Attorney

a Rule is allowed him to shew cause why the proceedings before the justice of the peace should be quashed.

Nathan Hawkins	)
VS	) Certio
William Britton	)

On motion of Plaintiff by Attorney a Rule is allowed him to shew cause why the Defendants petition and Writ should be dismissed -

James McCollum	)
VS	) Motion for Judgment for Monies paid as
Philip T. Babb	) Security

It appearing to the Satisfaction of the Court that the Plaintiff become Security for the Defendant for the payment of the costs of a State prosecution that in consequence of becoming Security as aforesaid he has been compelled to pay the sum of fourteen dollars - Therefore on motion of the plaintiff by James P. Taylor his attorney It is considered that he recover against the the Defendant the aforesaid Sum of fourteen Dollars and the costs of this motion -

                    (Fi Fa Issd. & Delivd. Plff. 5 Augt. 1826)
(P-89)   (To Greene County   )

Levi Babb	)
VS	) Motion for Judgment for Monies paid as
Philip T. Babb	) Security

It appearing to the Satisfaction of the court that the plaintiff become security for the Defendant for the payment of the costs of a State prosecution that in consequence of becoming Security as aforesaid he has been compelled to pay the sum of thirteen dollars ninety one and one fourth cents - Therefore on motion of the plaintiff by James P. Taylor his Attorney It is considered that the plaintiff recover against the Defendant the aforesaid sum of thirteen dollars ninety one and one fourth cents and the costs of this motion

Samuel Milliken	)
VS	) Motion for Judgmt. for monies paid as
Philip T. Babb	) Security.

It appearing to the Satisfaction of the Court that the plaintiff become security for the Defendant for the prosecution of a Writ of Certiorari that in consequence of becoming Security as aforesaid he has been compelled to pay the sum of fifteen dollars - Therefore on motion of the plaintiff It is considered by the court that the plaintiff recover against the Defendant the aforesaid sum of fifteen dollars and the costs of this motion.

(P-90)

John Baker)
  VS)   T.V.A.
Peter Brown,)
James McKinley,)   On motion of Plaintiff and with the
& Henry Dyche)   assent of Defendants Counsel ordered
    that the name of James McKinley be
struck from the Writ that the plaintiff may be enabled to
file his Declaration -

Richard Scruggs)
  VS) Debt
Daniel Cremer)
    The Defendant, in his proper person appear-
ed in Court and confessed that he owes the plaintiff the Sum
of Two Hundred Fifty Two Dollars and Forty Cents and his costs
by him about his Suit in this behalf expended -

State of Tennessee)
  VS)   Bastardy 2 Cases
James McKahan)
    On motion and with the assent of the
Court a Nolli Prosequi is entered and the costs of the same
assumed by the Defendant in his proper person. Therefore
it is considered that the State of Tennessee recover against
the said James McKeehan the costs aforesaid according to his
assumpsit and the fines in each case -

(P-91)

Ryan Woods)
  VS) Ca. Sa. Issued by a Justice
John Kesterson)
    The Defendant having been arrested by Virtue
of a Ca. Sa. issued by a Justice of the peace appeared accordingly and having taken the insolvent Debtors oath It is ordered thathe discharged and that the plaintiff pay the costs in
this behalf expended.

John Farnsworth)
  VS) Case in Trover
Isaac Baker)
    The plaintiff in his proper person appeared
in Court and dismissed his Suit and assumes the cost. Therefore it is considered that the Defendant recover against the
plaintiff his costs by him about his Suit in this behalf expended.

John Bewley, Assignee)
Nicholas Bragg) Debt
  vs.)
Hugh Maloney) This day came the plaintiff by Attor-
    ney and thereupon a jury to wit,

Samuel Henderson, John Thomason, James Kenney, Thomas Harvey, John Hybarger, William Thomason, Daniel Delany, Jacob Gass, Thomas Thomason, Jacob Hybarger, John Gass, Henry Fearle, who being elected tried and sworn well and truly to try this cause upon their oath do say that the Defendant has not paid the debt in the Declaration mentioned and assess the plaintiffs Damages by reason of (P-92) the Detention of that Debt to forty three Dollars. Therefore it is considered that the plaintiffs recover against the Defendant the sum of two hundred dollars the Debt in the declaration mentioned with the Damages aforesaid by the jury aforesaid assessed and his costs by him about his suit in this behalf expended -

Richard M. Woods esquire high Sheriff in and for the County of Greene returns here into open Court the States Writ of Venire Facias to him directed "Received and executed in full" A. M. Woods, Shff which said writ was endorsed "returnable Tuesday after the fourth Monday in July, Issd. 2nd. May 1826 - out of whom are elected as the Statutes in that case provides the following persons a Grand inquest and Jury that is to say -

Henry McAlpin appointed foreman by the Court.. William L. French, Benjamin Smith, Jacob Carter, Samuel Keller, James Moore, Joseph Melone, John Wright, Jacob Cobble, John Wallis, William Wykle, Jacob Wright, David Robertson, good and lawful men of the County of Greene who being now here empanelled and sworn to enquire for the State aforesaid and for the Body of the County of Greene aforesaid received their charge and retired from the Bar -

William Samples, a constable was qualified to attend on the above Jury 4 days.
                    Certificate Issd.

(P-93)   Jeremiah Farnsworth and Wyatt Hill the residue of the Venire to the present court are to attend the present Court as jurors untill discharged.

Turner Smith a Constable was appointed to attend on the Court 5 days, certificate issd. Wm. K. Vance

For satisfactory reasons appearing to the court Ordered that the following persons be discharged from further attendance at the present court to wit, Eliakim Cox, Vincent Anders on, Alexander Brown, John McCord, Samuel Hunter, John Bible, William Whittenberg, Peter Fry, John McCord, and Dutton Lane -

Nathaniel West, Assignee)
James W. Wyly   )   Motion for Judgment for failing
   vs   )   to return an execution the
Richard M. Woods a   )   plaintiff against John Low.
Constable and Securities   )

The plaintiff by Attorney moved the Court for judgment against the Defendant for failing to return an execution the plaintiff against John Low within Twenty days from the issuance thereof - which motion was ordered to be entered -

(This motion withdrawn by Sd. W. Wyly Plffs Atty.)

(P-94)

Martin Fry)
vs) Appeal.
Vincent Fry Applt.)

This day came the parties by attornies and thereupon a jury to wit Samuel Henderson, John Thomason, James Kenney, Thomas Harvey, John Hybarger, William Thomason, Daniel Delany, Jacob Gass, Thomas Thomason, Jacob Hybarger, John Gass and Henry Fearle who being elected tried and sworn well and truly to try this cause upon their oath do say that they find for the plaintiff three dollars - Therefore it is considered by the Court that the plaintiff recover against the Defendant and Zachariah Kinnamon security for the prosecution of his appeal the aforesaid sum of three dollars and his costs by him about his suit in this behalf expended -

Thomas Harvey)
vs) Certio
John Thomason)

This day came the parties by attornies and thereupon a jury to wit, Joseph Bradley, John Walker, Thomas Davis, Benjamin Anderson, Allen Ross, Levi Babb, Peter Swatsel, William Dunwoody, James Anderson, Samuel Milliken, Geo. Welty and Jacob Newman, who being elected, tried and sworn well and truly to try this cause returned to the Bar and declared they could not agree. Whereupon by consent or mistrial is entered and the jury from rendering their verdict discharged -

(P-95)

James McKeehan)
vs) Breach of prison Rules
Alexander Sevier)

On motion of James McKeehan by James W. Wyly his attorney against the said Alexander Sevier and Wm. Dickson his security on a Bond executed by them conditioned that the said Alexander Sevier who had been heretofore arrested on a Capias ad Satisfaciendum at the Suit of the plaintiff for the sum of ninety nine dollars forty and one half cents should keep within the prison Rules of the County of Greene and it appearing to the Satisfaction of the court that the said Alexander Sevier has escaped from the prison Rules of this County and that the Defendants have been served with notice of this motion as is required by the act of assembly__ Whereupon it is considered by the court that the plaintiff recover against the said Alexander Sevier and William Dickson has security as aforesaid the said sum of ninety nine dollars forty and one half cents with interest thereon from the sixth day of November one thousand eight hundred and twenty four at the rate of Six per cent pr. annum up to the

present time - with the Sum of three dollars and fifteen
cents, the costs accruing on the original suit and the costs
of this motion -

(P-96
James McKeehan   )
        VS   )   Breach of prison Rules
Alexander Sevier and   )
William Dickson   )   On motion of James McKeehan, by
his Security   )   James W. Wyly his Attorney for a
                            judgment against the said Alexander
Sevier and William Dickson his Security on a Bond executed
by them conditioned that the said Alexander Sevier who had
been heretofore arrested on a Capias ad Satisfaciendum at
the Suit of the plaintiff for the Sum of fifty dollars and
fifty seven cents debt and three dollars and fifteen cents
costs should keep within the prison rules of the county of
Greene and it appearing to the satisfaction of the court that
the said Alexander Sevier has escaped from the prison Rules
of said County and that the Defendants have been served with
notice of this motion as is required by the act of assembly -
Whereupon it is considered by the court that the plaintiff
recover against the said Alexander Sevier and William Dickson
the aforesaid sum of fifty dollars and fifty seven cents, with
interest thereon at the rate of Six pr. cent pr annum from
the sixth day of November one thousand eight hundred and
Twenty four - with the Sum of three dollars and fifteen cents
the costs accruing on the original suit and the costs of this
motion -

(P-97)
Stephen Smith   )
    VS.   )   Order Sale
John M. Kilgore)
        John McBride, a Deputy Sheriff of Greene
County returned here into court on execution issued by Wm.
McBride, esquire an acting justice of the peace for said
county against the estate of the Defendant for the sum of
five dollars and seventy two cents debt and fifty cents cost
recovered by the plaintiff against the Defendant before said
justice on the 23rd. day of January 1826. on which execution
said Sheriff has made return. Search made and no personal
property found in my county this execution levied 26th. June
1826 on a tract of land the property of John M. Kilgore, containing twenty five acres joining John Stephens, John Renner,
and John Coggburn Therefore on motion of the plaintiff It
is considered by the Court thatthe aforesaid Tract of Land
so levied on be condemned to the Satisfaction of the Recovery
aforesaid and that the same or so much thereof as will satisfy said Recovery and the costs of this motion be sold as the
law directs -

        And Court adjourned untill tomorrow morning 9 o'clock.
                                A. Gillespie
                                H. D. Hale
                                Lewis Ball

(P-98)   Wednesday 26th. July 1826.

Court met present

The Minutes of Yesterdays proceedings were read and
signed.

Hugh Malony   )   Motion for Judgment for Monies paid as
    vs.   )   Security
Benjamin White   )
                      It appearing to the satisfaction of the court
that the plaintiff become Security for the Defendant in a
note given to Nicholas Bragg that in consequence of becoming
Security aforesaid he has been compelled to pay the sum of
Two hundred fifty three dollars sixty two and one half cents -
Therefore on motion of the plaintiff by Robert I. McKinney
his attorney, It is considered by the Court that the plaintiff recover against the Defendant the aforesaid Sum of Two
hundred and fifty three dollars sixty two and one half cents
and the costs of this motion -

State of Tennessee)
Jno. Bowman Pros.)
    vs.   )   T. A. B.
Leonard Rush   )
                      This day came as well the Attorney Gen-
eral as the Defendant in his proper person- and the Defendant
withdrawing the plea of not guilty confesses that he is
(P-99)   guilty in manner and form as charged in the Bill
of Indictment. Therefore it is considered by the Court that
the Defendant for such his offence be fined forfeit and pay
to the State of Tennessee the Sum of fifty cents and he pay
the costs of this prosecution - And thereupon came Willis
Norton and Thomas Rush and assumed for & on behalf of the
defendant the payment of the Fine and costs aforesaid and
agree that judgment be entered against him for the same.
Therefore it is considered that the State of Tennessee recover
against the said Willis Norton and Thomas Rush the costs
aforesaid according to their assumpsit.

State of Tennessee)
    vs   )   T. A. B. on Philip Bird
Howell Houston   )
                      This day came as well the Attorney
General as the Attorney General as the Defendant in his
proper person and the Defendant being charged on the Bill
of indictment for plea thereto says that he is not guilty
in manner and form as charged in the bill of indictment
and puts himself on the County and the Attorney General
having done the like came also a jury to wit, Charles Dyche
Jacob Starnes, George Kerbough, William Mitchell, Charles
Nichols, William Wisecarner, Pleasant Hill, John Thomason
Edward Y. Russell, Samuel Walker, Leland Davis and Henry
Humbard who being elected tried and sworn well and truly

to try this cause upon their oath do say that the Defendant
is guilty in manner and form as charged in (P-100) the
Bill of Indictment. Therefore it is considered that the
Defendant for such his offence be fined forfeit and pay
to the State of Tennessee the sum of five Dollars and that
he pay the costs of this prosecution -

State of Tennessee   )
Thomas H. Wilson, Prosr.)   T. A. B.
        VS.   )
Charles Dyche   )   This day came as well theAttor-
                                ney General as. the Defendant
in his proper person and the Defendant being charged on the
Bill of Indictment for plea says that he is not guilty in
manner and form as charged in the Bill of Indictment and
puts himself on the Country and the Attorney General having
done the same came also a jury to wit, Jeremiah Farnsworth
Wyatt Hill, William Smith, William Britton, George Ackerson,
Jacob Newman, Peter Swatsel, Jacob Steele, Dutton Lane,
Frederick F. Winkle, Thomas Dodd and Benjamin Wampler who
being elected tried and sworn the truth to speak upon this
issue of traverse upon their oath do say that the Defendant
is guilty in manner and form as charged in the Bill of Indictment - therefore it is considered that the Defendant for
such his offence be fined forfeit and pay to the State of
Tennessee the sum of Twenty five cents and that he pay the
costs of this prosecution -

(P-101)
State of Tennessee)
Amos Garrett Prosr.)
    VS.   )
George Freshour   )
                    Continued as on affidavit of Defendant
George Freshour acknowledged to owe the State of Tennessee
one hundred dollars and John Freshour and Howell Houston his
Sureties also acknowledged to owe the State the Sum of fifty
Dollars each - Yet upon condition that if George Freshour
shall make his personal appearance at the Court of Pleas and
Quarter Sessions to be held for the County of Greene in the
Courthouse in Greeneville on Wednesday next after the fourth
Monday in October next and stand his trial in this prosecution
against him and not depart the court without leave then the
above recognizance to be void otherwise in force -

State of Tennessee   )
John McCurry, Pros.   )   T. A. B.
    VS.   )
William Blair   )   This day came as well the Attorney
                            General as the Defendant in his
proper person and the Defendant being charged on the Bill of
Indictment for plea thereto says that he is not guilty in
manner and form as therein against him is alledged and puts
himself on the Country and the Attorney General having done

the like came also a jury to wit Erwin Allison, John Walker
Ironymus Dyche, Leonard Rush, John Bowman, Michael Maltsberger, Jacob Garrett, Emanuel Dyche, John Cook, Jacob Hybarger
Jeremiah Casteel, and Daniel Benson, who being elected tried
(P-102) and sworn well and truly to try this cause upon their
oath do say that the Defendant is not guilty in manner and
form as charged in the bill of indictment -

And on motion - Ordered that the costs of this prosecution be paid by the Trustee of Greene County.

State of Tennessee   )
Harvey Williams, Pros.   )   T. A. B.
        vs.   )
William Green   )   This day came as well the Attorney
                                 General as the Defendant in his
proper person and the Defendant being charged on the Bill of
Indictment for plea says that he is guilty in manner and form
as therein against him is alledged and puts himself on the
mercy of the Court - Therefore it is considered that the Defendant for such his offence be fined forfeit and pay to the
State of Tennessee the sum of fifty cents and that he pay the
costs of this prosecution - and is charged in custody of the
Sheriff untill fine and costs are paid.

State of Tennessee &   )
Abraham Sellers   )   Peace Warrant
        vs   )
Jacob Stiegel   )   Jacob Stiegel acknowledged to owe
                                the State of Tennessee one hundred
Dollars and Michael Maltsberger his Surety also acknowledged
to owe the State of Tennessee the sum of fifty dollars - Yet
upon (P-103) condition that if Jacob Stiegel shall keep
the peace towards all the good people of the State of Tenn.
for the space of three months from the present time but especially towards Abraham Sellers - then the recognizance to be
void otherwise in force whereupon it is ordered that the said
Jacob Stiegel pay the costs in this behalf expended -

State of Tennessee   )
Solomon Sellers, Prosr.)
        vs.   )   T. A. B.
David Millburn, Junr.   )
                                This day came as well the Attorney
General as the Defendant in his proper person and the Defendant being charged on the Bill of Indictment for plea thereto
says that he is not guilty in manner and form as therein against
him is alledged and puts himself on the Country and the Attorney General having done the same came also a jury to wit
Jeremiah Farnsworth, Wyatt Hill, William Smith, William Britton, Peter Swatsel, Dutton Lane, Frederick T. Winkle, Benjamin
Wampler, Daniel Britton, John Gass, (of James), Evans McNeese,
and Joseph Hunter, who being elected tried and sworn the truth
to speak upon this issue of Traverse upon their oath do say
that the Defendant is guilty in manner and form as charged in

the bill of Indictment. Therefore it is considered that
the Defendant for such his offence be fined forfeit and pay
to the State of Tennessee the Sum of Twenty Five cents and
that he pay the costs of this prosecution and is charged
in custody of the Sheriff untill fine and costs are paid.

(P-104)
State of Tennessee   )
Abraham Sellers, Prosr.   )
      vs.   )   T. A. B.
Jacob Stiegel   )

                This day came as well the Attorney
General as the Defendant in his proper person and the Defendant being charged on the bill of Indictment for plea thereto
says that he is not guilty in manner and form as therein
against him is alledged and puts himself on the Country and
the Attorney General having do the same came also a jury to
wit Jeremiah Farnsworth, Wyatt Hill, William Smith, William
Britton, Peter Swatsel, Dutton Lane, Frederick T. Winkle,
Benjamin Wampler, Daniel Britton, John Gass, Evans McNeese,
and Joseph Hunter who being elected tried and sworn the truth
to speak upon this issue of traverse upon their oath do say
that the Defendant is guilty in manner and form as charged
in the Bill of Indictment. Therefore it is considered that
the Defendant for such his offence be fined forfeet and pay
to the State of Tennessee the Sum of one cent and that he
pay the costs of this prosecution -
* (See page 62A. for next Article)
John Baker   )
      vs.   ) Certio
Howell Houston and   )
William Houston   )

                Commissioners are awarded the plaintiff
to take the depositions of Jacob Baker and Absalom Houston of
Monroe County - Commissioners are also awarded the Defendants
to take the Depositions of James Baker, Jacob Baker and Absalom Houston, of Monroe County which commissions may be directed
to anyone justice of the peace for said county of Monroe -
The parties giving each other twenty days notice of the time
and place of executing such commissions -

State of Tennessee   )
Gross Scruggs, Prosr.   )   T.A.B.
      vs.   )
Ryon Woods   )   This day came as well the Attorney
                   General as the Defendant in his
proper person and the Defendant being charged on the Bill
of Indictment for plea thereto says that he is guilty in
manner and form as therein against his alledged and puts
himself on the mercy of the court. Therefore itis considered
by the court that the Defendant for such his offence be fined
forfeit and pay to the State of Tennessee the sum of one cent
and that he pay the costs of this prosecution - And thereupon
came Gideon Bryant and assured for and on behalf of the Defendant

Thomas Harvey)
    vs.) Certio
John Thomason)

       By consent the matters in dispute between
the parties in this suit are refered to the final determination of David Rankin, Cornelius Smith, Benjamin Carter and
William A. Hankins with liberty to choose a fifth Referee
in case they should not   (P-105)   agree whose acused thereupon is to be made the judgment of the Court which is ordered
accordingly.

the payment of the fine and costs aforesaid and agrees that judgment be entered against him for the same - Therefore it is   (P-106.)   considered that the State of Tennessee recover against the said Gideon Bryant the fine and cost aforesaid according to his assumpsit -

State of Tennessee   )
Richard M. Woods, Prosr.   )   Indict for Pettet Larceny
        vs.   )
Elisabeth McNew   )   On motion and with the assent of
                                   the court a Nolli Prosequi is
entered in this prosecution the costs of which are assumed by the Defendants Securities. Therefore it is considered that the State of Tennessee recover against James W. Wyly John Hays, John Guin, Henry Garrett, Thomas Battersby, Seth I. W. Luckey, William E. Gillespie, F. T. Gillespie, Hosekiah B. Wyly, James McClanyhan, Samuel White, George Broadway, and Jacob T. Wyrick the costs of this prosecution according to their assumpsit -

State of Tennessee)
        vs.   )   Bastardy
Cross Scruggs   )
                        Issue made up to try whether the Defendant is the father of a Bastard child charged on him by Edith Woods or not.
        This day came as well the Attorney General as the Defendant by his Counsel and thereupon the issue made up in this prosecution came on to be heard and Determined by the Court. Whereupon all and singular the premises being seen and by the Court fully understood. It is considered and adjudged by the court that the said Cross Scruggs is the father of the child charged on him,   (P-107)   by Edith Woods - and it is further considered and ordered by the court that the said Cross Scruggs enter into Bond with approved Security for the maintenance of said child and that he pay the costs in this behalf expended - and also the Fine -

State of Tennessee)
        vs.   )   Bastardy
William Benham   )
                        The Defendant who stands bound by recognizance for his appearance here to answer the State of Tennessee of a charge alledged against him for begeting a Bastard child of the body of Polly Darrow of this County single woman - appeared accordingly - And Nancy Benham and James Davis entered into Bond in the Sum of five hundred Dollars conditioned that the said William Benham (a Minor) shall perform such order as the Court from time to time shall make concerning the maintenance of said child, and indemnify the County of Greene free from all Charges in consequence of the Birth and maintenance of said child -

Whereupon it is ordered that the said William Benham pay
the costs in this behalf expended -

John Kifer   )
    vs.   )   Attachment
The Estate of   )
Thomas Davis   ) The plaintiff in his proper person dismisses
his Attachment and assumes the cost - Therefore it is considered that the plaintiff pay the costs in this behalf expended (P-108) and Court adjourned untill tomorrow morning
9 o'clock.
                    Henry Dyche
                    M. Lincoln
                    Hugh D. Hale

      Thursday 27th. July 1826
      Court met present

      The Minutes of yesterdays proceedings were read and
signed.

State of Tennessee)
    vs.   )   Sci Fa Forfeited
Hugh Malony Bail recog.)
of Gross Scruggs   )   On motion and with the assent
                      of Court the forfeiture in this
Writ of Scire Facias named is set aside and the costs thereof
assumed by the Defendant. Therefore it is considered that
the State of Tennessee recover against the said Hugh Malony
the costs expended in sueing forth and prosecuting the States
Writ of Scire Facias -
(P-109)

State of Tennessee)
    vs.   )   Sci Fa Forfeited Recogs. Bail
Robert McKenny   )
  of Gross Scrugs) On motion and with the assent of the court
                      the forfeiture in this Writ of Scire
Facias named is set aside and the costs thereof assumed by
Hugh Malony for the Defendant - Therefore it is considered
that the State of Tennessee recover against the Defendant
and the said Hugh Malony the costs expended in sueing forth
and presenting the States Writ of Scire Facias -

State of Tennessee)
    vs.   ) Bastardy
Thomas Dodd   )
      The Defendant who stand bound by recog-
nisance for his appearance here to answer the State of Tennessee of a charge alledged against him for beget-ing a
Bastard child of the body of Phoebe King of this County
single woman appeared according by and thereupon Phoebe King
and Michael Myers entered into bond in the sum of five hundred Dollars conditioned that the said Phoebe King shall
perform such order as the Court from time to time shall

make concerning the maintenance of said child and indemnify the County of Greene free from all charges in consequence of the Birth and maintenance of said child - Whereupon it is ordered that the said Phoebe King pay the costs in this behalf expended -

(P-110)

State of Tennessee)
John Oliphant, Prosr.) Indict for Pettit Larceny
    vs)
John Collett of Jacob) This day came as well the Attorney
                             General as the Defendant in his proper person and by his counsel and the Defendant being charged on the Bill of Indictment for plea thereto says that he is not guilty in manner and form as charged in the Bill of Indictment and puts himself on the Country and the Attorney General having done the same came also a jury to wit Jeremiah Farns - worth, Wyatt Hill, John Parsons, Jacob Garrett, Thomas Dodd, William Smith, Leland Davis, William Grant, William Pogue, David Farnsworth, Nathaniel D. Moore, and Ellett Rutherford who being elected tried and sworn the truth to speak upon this issue of traverse upon their oath do say that the Defendant is guilty in manner and form as charged in the Bill of Indictment Therefore it is considered by the Court that the said John Collett for the offence aforesaid be commited to the common jail of Greene County thereto remain untill tomorrow at twelve of the clock, at which time the said John Collett, shall be taken to the public whipping post and there receive twenty lashes on his bare back, and that he pay the costs of this prosecution and be returned in custody of the sheriff untill the same are paid.

From which judgment the Defendant by Attorney prays an appeal to the next circuit court to be held for the County of Greene in the Courthouse in Greenville on the first Monday in September next.

(P-111)

State of Tennessee)
and Peter Sellers) Surety of the Peace Required.
    vs) Peter Sellers having made oath that
David Millburn, Junr.) he is in fear of his life or some
                             bodily hurt to be done or procured to be done him by David Millburn, Junr. and that he does not require the peace of him for any malice Hexation or revengs but for the cause aforesaid - It is ordered that the said Defendant find Sureties of the peace which he failing to do, It is ordered that he be commited to the common jail of Greene County there to remain untill such Security be given.

Simon Gentry)
    vs) Order Sale
John Fincher)
                Turner Smith a constable of Greene County returned here into Court an execution issued by Cornelius Smith esquire an acting justice of the peace for said County

against the estate of the Defendant for the Sum of forty
Six dollars fifty two and a half cents Debt and fifty cents
cost recovered by the plaintiff against the defendant before
said justice on the 15th. day of June 1826 on which execution said constable has made return Search made and no goods
or chattels of the Defendant found in my County and levied
on one hundred and sixty acres of land the property (P-112)
of John Fincher adjoining lands of Robert K. Pickens, Alexander English and William Hays so returned by me this 30th.
June 1826.
        Turner Smith Constable.
    Therefore on motion of the plaintiff it is considered
that the aforesaid tract of land so levied on be condemned
to the satisfaction of the recovery aforesaid and that the
same or so much thereof as will satisfy said recovery and
the costs of this motion be sold as the law directs -

    An assignment from Lewis Morgan to George House of a
plat and certificate of Survey of No. 254 was duly acknowledged by the said Thomas Morgan and is as follows
      July 27th. 1826. I assign over the within plat
      and certificate to George House it being for value
      received of him witness my hand and Seal
                Thomas Morgan (LS)
Attest
James Patterson

    An assignment from Lewis Morgan to George House of a
plat and certificate of survey of No. 255 was duly acknowledged by the said Lewis Morgan and is as follows
      July 27th. 1826. I assign over the within plat and
      certificate of survey to George House being for value
      accord of him.
            Witness my hand and Seal
               Lewis Morgan (L.S.)
Attest
James Patterson

(P-113)   And Court adjourned untill tomorrow morning 9
       O'clock
                Henry Dyche
                Joseph Brown
                Leonard Starnes
    Friday 28th. July 1826 Court met present

    The Minutes of yesterdays proceedings were read and
signed. -

State of Tennessee   )
John Oliphant, Prosr.)   Indict for Pettit Larceny
   vs   )
John Collett of Jacob)   On motion and for Satisfactory
                    reasons appearing reasons appear -
ing to the Court the punishment ordered to be inflicted on
the Defendant on yesterday is reduced to five lashes and the

Sheriff of Greene County is ordered to execute the judgment
of the Court at 10 o'clock of the present day and thereupon
came Jacob Collett and assumed for and on behalf of the
Defendant the payment of the costs of this (P-114) prosecution and agrees that judgment be entered against him for the
same. Therefore it is considered that the State of Tennessee
recover against the said Jacob Collett the costs of this prosecution according to his assumpsit

Execution staid 3 months

State of Tennessee)
vs) Forft. Recogd.
Alexander Sevier)
Bail of Gross Scruggs) On motion ordered that the forfeiture
in this writ of Scire Facias named be
set aside - and the costs of the same are assumed by the Defendant in his proper person - Therefore it is considered that the
State of Tennessee recover against the Defendant the costs expended in sueing forth and presenting the States Writ of Scire
Facias -

James P. Taylor)
vs.) Order Sale
Christopher Cooper, Junr) Thomas Dodd, a constable of Greene
County returned here into court on
execution issued by Isaac Justis esquire an acting justice of
the peace for said County against the estate of the Defendant
for the sum of five dollars and fifteen cents Debt and fifty
cents costs recorded by the plaintiff against the Defendant
before said justice on the 27th. day of April 1826 on which
execution said constable has made return "Search made (P-115)
no personal property to be found that said Cooper claims levied on seven acres of land belonging to said Christopher Cooper
adjoining lands with Edmond Casteel and including part of the
land occupied by Zaphar Johnson Junr. July 21st. 1826 returned
by me, Thomas Dodd Constable.

Therefore on motion of the said James P. Taylor, it is
considered that the aforesaid tract of land be condemned to
the satisfaction of the recovery aforesaid and that the same
or so much thereof as will satisfy said recovery and the costs
of this motion be sold as the law directs --

Thomas Stroud)
vs.) Certio
William Bowling)
This day came the parties by Attornies and
thereupon a jury to wit Jeremiah Farnsworth, Wyatt Hill,
Jacob Newman, Thomas Thomason, Peter Sellers, Harvey Wilson,
Daniel Guin, Peter Swatsel, Daniel M. Guin, Eliakim Cox,
Absalom Haworth, John Maltsberger Junr. who being elected
tried and sworn well and truly to try this cause upon their
oath do say that they find for the plaintiff forty three dollars. -

And on motion of Defendant by Attorney a Rule is
allowed him to shew cause why a new trial should
be granted - Whereupon all and singular the pre -
mises being seen and by the Court fully understood
It is considered that said rule be made absolute.

(P-116)

State of Tennessee)
Jacob Stiegel prosr.)   T. A. B. on David Millburn
        vs.)
William Wicker)   This day came as well the Attorney
                        General as the Defendant in his pro-
per person and the Defendant being charged on the Bill of
Indictment for plea says that he is not guilty in manner and
form as therein against him is alledged and puts himself on
the Country and the Attorney General having done the same
came also a jury to wit, James Hise, John Oliphant William
Britton, James Bailey, Benjamin Swatsel, William McAmish,
Samuel Lauderdale, Edward Y. Russell, Isaac Harmon, James
McAmish , Abraham Bowen and Thomas Batt who being elected
tried and sworn the truth to speak upon this issue of Traverse upon their oath do say that the Defendant is guilty
in manner and form as charged in the Bill of Indictment
Therefore it is considered that the Defendant for such his
offence be fined forfeit and pay to the State of Tennessee
the Sum of one Dollar and that he pay the costs of this
prosecution - and thereupon came Peter Sellers and William
L. French and assumed for and on behalf of the Defendant the
payment of the Fine and costs aforesaid and agree that judgment be entered against them for the same - Therefore it is
considered that the State of Tennessee recover against the
said Peter Sellers and William L. French the costs aforesaid
according to their assumpsit.

(P-117)

State of Tennessee)
Jacob Stiegel, prosr.)   Indict for aiding & assisting
        vs)   in T. A. B. on David Millburn
Solomon Sellers)
                        This day came as well the Attorney
General as the Defendant in his proper person and the Defendant being charged on the Bill of Indictment for plea thereto says that he is guilty in manner and form as therein against him is alledged and puts himself on the mercy of the Court
Therefore It is considered that the Defendant for such his
offence be fined forfeit and pay to the State of Tennessee
the sum of one dollar and that he pay the costs of this prosecution - and thereupon came William L. French and Peter
Sellers and assumed for and on behalf of the Defendant the
payment of the fine and costs aforesaid and agree that judgment be entered against them for the same Therefore it is
considered that the State of Tennessee recover against the
said William L French and Peter Sellers and assumed for and
on behalf of the Defendant the payment of the fine and costs
aforesaid and agree that judgment be entered against them for

the same Therefore it is considered that the State of Tennessee recover against the said William L. French and Peter Sellers the costs aforesaid according to their assumpsit.

State of Tennessee   )
           vs   )   Bastardy
Joshua Bowling, Junr.)

                     The Defendant who stands bound by recognisance for his appearance here to answer the State of Tennessee of a charge alledged against him for begeting a Bastard child of the body of Mary Ann Dornikin of this County single woman appeared accordingly and entered into bond in the sum of six hundred dollars conditioned that (P-118) the said Joshua Bowling Junr. shall perform such order as the Court from time to time shall make concerning the maintenance of said child and indemnify the County of Greene free from all charges in consequence of the Birth and maintenance of said child - Whereupon it is ordered that the said Joshua Bowling Junr. pay the costs in this behalf expended - And thereupon Joshua Bowling Junr. in his proper person appeared in court and assumed for and on behalf of the Defendant the payment of the costs aforesaid and agrees that judgment be entered against him for the same - Therefore it is considered that the State of Tennessee recover against the said Joshua Bowling Senr. the costs aforesaid according to his assumpsit and also the Fine six dollars and twenty five cents -

State of Tennessee   )
George Jones, Prosr.)   Indict. for Pettit Larceny
      vs   )
James Felts, Deft.   )   This day came as well the Attorney
                     General as the Defendant in his proper person and the Defendant being charged on the Bill of Indictment for plea thereto says that he is not guilty in manner and form as therein against him is alledged and puts himself on the Country and the Attorney General having done the same came also a jury to wit, Jacob Stiegel, William Bowling, Stephens Massey, John Harmon, Andrew Park, James Bailey, Dutton Lane, George H. Starnes, Absalom Thompson, Jacob Rimel, Henry A. Farnsworth and John Thomason, who being elected tried and sworn the truth to speak upon this issue of traverse upon their oath do say that the Defendant (P-119) is guilty in manner and form as charged in the Bill of Indictment. Therefore it is considered by the Court that the said James Felts for the offence aforesaid be taken to the public whiping post and there receive five lashes on his bare back which sentence the Sheriff of Greene County is ordered to carry into immediate execution - and it is also ordered that the said Defendant pay the costs of this prosecution - and thereupon James Felts Senr. in his proper person appeared in court and assumed for and on behalf of the Defendant the payment of the costs aforesaid and agrees that judgment be entered against him for the same. Therefore it is considered that the State of Tennessee recover against the said James

Felts Senr. the costs aforesaid according to his assumpsit –

William Ballard, assignee)
David C. Posey) Cont. Writ of Enquiry
vs)
Hiram Hogan) This day came the plaintiff by
attorney and thereupon a jury
to wit, Jeremiah Farnsworth, Wyatt Hill, William Luster,
Thomas Thomason, Peter Sellers, Harvey Wilson, Eliakim Cox,
Absalom Haworth, Peter Swatsel, Daniel M. Guin, John Maltsberger and Daniel Delany who being elected tried and sworn
well and truly to enquire of Damages between the parties
upon their oath do say that the plaintiff has sustained
Damages by occasion in the Declaration mentioned to one hundred and five dollars and fifty cents. Therefore it is
considered that the plaintiff recover against the Defendant
the Damages aforesaid by the jury aforesaid assessed and his
costs by   (P-120) him about his suit in this behalf expended

State of Tennessee)
Jacob Stiegel prosr.) Indict. for aiding and assisting
vs.) in T. A. B. on David Millburn
Abraham Sellers)
This day came as well the Attorney
General as the Defendant in his proper person and the Defendant being charged on the Bill of Indictment for plea thereto
says that he is not guilty in manner and form as therein
against him is alledged and puts himself on the Country and
the Attorney General having done the same came also a jury
to wit Jeremiah Farnsworth, Wyatt Hill, William Luster, Thomas Thomason, Harvey Wilson, Eliakim Cox, Absalom Haworth,
Peter Swatsel, Daniel Delany, William Johnson, Andrew Roberts
and James Guin who being elected tried and sworn the truth
to speak upon this issue of Traverse upon their oath do say
that the Defendant is not guilty in manner and form as charged
in the bill of Indictment –
And on motion and for satisfactory reasons appearing
to the Court ordered that the costs of this prosecution
be paid by the Trustee of Greene County

State of Tennessee)
and Ira Green) Surety of the peace required
vs)
Jacob Hise) The prosecutor, Ira Green failing to
appear it is ordered by the Court that
the Defendant be discharged and that Ira Green pay the costs
in this behalf expended.
(P-121)   Grand & Pettit Jurors discharged 4 days.

Valentine Sevier for the)
use of Thomas Crutchfield) Debt
vs)
Alexander Sevier) This day came the parties
by attornies and thereupon
a jury to wit Jacob Stiegel, John Harmon, Andrew Park, James

Bailey, Dutton Lane, George A. Starnes, Absalom Thompson, Henry A. Farnsworth, John Thomason, Harvey Williams, Enos Pickering and Hesekiah Hughes who being elected tried and sworn the truth to speak upon the issue joined upon their oath do say that the Defendant has not paid the Debt in the Declaration mention as in pleading he hath alledged and they do assess the plaintiffs Damages by reason of the Detention of that Debt to Twelve Dollars and twenty five cents. Therefore it is considered that the plaintiff recover against the Defendant the Sum of three hundred fifty Dollars eighty two cents the Debt in the Declaration mentioned with the Damages by the jury aforesaid assessed and his costs by him about his suit in this behalf expended -

Isaac Baker)
   vs)   Certio
Jacob Rimall)

    This day came the parties by attornies and thereupon a jury to wit Jacob Stiegel, John Harmon, Andrew Park, James Bailey, Dutton Lane, George/Henry A. Farnsworth, John Thomason, Harvey (P-122) Williams, Enos Pickering and Hesekiah Hughes who being elected tried and sworn well and truly to try this cause upon their oath do say that they find for the Defendant- Therefore it is considered that the plaintiff take nothing by his suit but for his false clamor he in mercy &c. and that the Defendant go hence and recover against the Plaintiff his costs by him about his Defence in this behalf expended - * George H. Starnes, Absalom Thompson

Christopher Lotspeich)
   vs)   Debt Specie
Alexander Sevier and)
David Rice)

    This day came the parties by attornies and thereupon a jury to wit Jacob Stiegel, John Harmon, Andrew Park, James Bailey, Dutton Lane, George H. Starnes, Absalom Thompson, Henry A. Farnsworth John Thomason, Harvey Williams, Enos Pickering, and Hesekiah Hughes who being elected tried and sworn the truth to speak upon the issue joined upon their oath do say that the Defendants have not paid the Debt in the Declaration mentioned as in pleading they have alledged and they do assess the plaintiffs Damages by reason of the Detention of that debt to one hundred and twenty two dollars and fifty cents. Therefore it is considered by the court that the plaintiff recover against the Defendants the sum of one thousand dollars the debt in the Declaration mentioned with the Damages by the jury aforesaid assessed and his costs by him about his suit in this behalf expended -

(P-123)
George Smith, Assignee)
  James W. Wyly)   Covenant
   vs.)
James Allen)
    This day came the parties by attornies and thereupon a jury to wit

Jacob Stiegel, John Harmon, Andrew Park, James Bailey, Dutton Lane, George H. Starnes, Absalom Thompson, Henry A. Farnsworth John Thomason, Harvey Williams, Enos Pickering and Hesekiah Hughes who being elected tried and sworn the truth to speak upon the issue joined upon their oath do say that the Defendant hath not kept and performed his covenant as in pleading he hath alledged but hath broken the same in manner and form as the plaintiff against him in his Declaration hath complained and they do assess the plaintiffs damages by occasion thereof to one hundred and four dollars and seventeen cents. Therefore it is considered by the court that the plaintiff recover against the Defendant the Damages aforesaid by the jury aforesaid assessed and his costs by him about his suit in this behalf expended execution staid 5 months.

Joseph Rawlings)
    vs   ) T. V. A.
Abel Rymal)

    The plaintiff by his Attorney dismisses his suit and the Defendant in his proper person appeared in Court and assumed the cost. Therefore it is considered that the plaintiff recover against the Defendant his costs by him about his suit in this behalf expended –

(P-124)
State of Tennessee)
  Ira Green, prosr.)   Assault
    vs   )
Jacob Hise)   On motion and cause shewn by affidavit
               of James P. Taylor esquire this prosecution is continued untill the next court and thereupon Jacob Hise acknowledged to owe the State of Tennessee one hundred dollars and James Hise his Surety also acknowledged to owe the State of Tennessee fifty dollars yet upon condition that if Jacob Hise shall make his personal appearance at the Court of Pleas and Quarter Sessions to be held for the County of Greene in the Courthouse in Greeneville on Wednesday next after the fourth Monday in October next and stand his trial in this prosecution against him and not depart the court without leave then this recognisance to be void otherwise in force –

    And thereupon Ira Green who stands bound by recognisance, in the Sum of Two hundred Dollars for his appearance here to prosecute and give evidence on behalf of the State of Tennessee in this prosecution against Jacob Hise was solemnly called for that purpose but came not and made Default Therefore it is considered that the State of Tennessee recover against the said Ira Green the sum of Two Hundred Dollars the amount of his recognisance in this behalf acknowledged unless sufficient cause for such failure be shewn – Levi Babb, who stands bound by recognisance in the sum of one hundred dollars for the appearance here of Ira Greene to prosecute and give evidence (P-125) on behalf of the State of Tennessee was solemnly called to bring into court the body of the said Ira Green and

surrender the same in discharge of himself as Bail but failed
so to do and made default. Therefore it is considered that the
State of Tennessee recover against the said Levi Babb the sum
of one hundred dollars the amount of his recognisance in this
behalf acknowledged unless sufficient cause for such failure
be shewn -

State of Tennessee)
  Ira Green, prosr.)   Assault.
    vs)
Jacob Hise)   On motion and cause shewn by affidavit
             of James P. Taylor esquire this prose-
cution is continued untill next court and thereupon Jacob Hise
acknowledged to owe the State of Tennessee the sum of one hundred dollars and James Hise his Surety also acknowledged to
owe the State of Tennessee the sum of fifty dollars - yet upon
condition that if Jacob Hise shall make his personal appearance at the Court of Pleas and Quarter Sessions to be held for
the County of Greene in the Court house in Greeneville on
Wednesday next after the fourth Monday in October next and
and stand his trial in this prosecution against him and not
depart the Court without leave then the above recognisance to
be void otherwise in force -
    And thereupon Ira Green who stands bound by recognisance
in the Sum of two hundred dollars for his appearance here to
prosecute and give evidence on behalf of the State of Tennessee
in this prosecution against Jacob Hise   (P-126) was solemnly called for that purpose but came not and made Default.
Therefore it is considered that the State of Tennessee recover
against the said Ira Greene the sum of two hundred dollars
the amount of his recognisance in this behalf acknowledged
unless sufficient cause for such failure be shewn - Levi Babb
who stands bound by recognisance in the sum of one hundred
dollars for the appearance here of Ira Greene to prosecute
and give evidence on behalf of the State of Tennessee in this
prosecution against Jacob Hise was solemnly called to bring
into court the body of the said Ira Greene and surrender the
same in discharge of himself as bail but failed so to do,
Whereupon it is considered that the State of Tennessee recover
against the said Levi Babb the sum of one hundred dollars the
amount of his recognisance in this behalf acknowledged unless
sufficient cause be shewn -

State of Tennessee)
  Moses Johnson, pros.)   Assault
    vs)
James Long)   The Defendant who stands bound by
             recognisance in the sum of thirty
dollars for his appearance have to answer the State of Tennessee of a charged alledged against him for an assault offered
to Moses Johnson was solemnly called for that purpose but
came not and made default Therefore it is considered that the
State of Tennessee recover against the said James Long the sum
of thirty dollars the amount of his recognisance in this behalf

acknowledged unless sufficient cause be shewn (P-127) for such failure - John Long and Moses Johnson who stand bound by recognisance in the sum of fifteen dollars each for the appearance here of James Long to answer the State of Tennessee of a charge alledged against him for an assault offered to Moses Johnson were severally solemnly called to bring into Court the Body of the said James Long and surrender the same in discharge of themselves as bail but failed so to do and made default. Therefore it is considered that the State of Tennessee recover against the said John Long and Moses Johnson the sum of fifteen dollars each the amount of their several recognisance in this behalf acknowledged unless sufficient cause be shewn for such failure -

State of Tennessee)
  Moses Johnson, prosr.)   Indict for Blasphemy
    vs.)
James Long)   The Defendant who stands bound
                                  by recognisance in the sum of
one hundred dollars for his appearance here to answer the State of Tennessee of a charge alledged against him for the commission of Blasphemy was solemnly called for that purpose but came not and made default Therefore it is considered that the State of Tennessee recover against the said James Long the sum of one hundred dollars the amount of his recognisance in this behalf acknowledged unless sufficient cause for such failure be shewn - John Long and Moses Johnson who stand bound by recognisance in the sum of fifty dollars each for the appearance here of James Long Long to answer the State of Tennessee; of a charge alledged against him for the (P-128) commission of a Blasphemy were severally solemnly called to bring into court the body of the said James Long and surrender the same in discharge of themselves as bail but failed so to do and made Default - Therefore it is considered that the State of Tennessee recover against the said John Long and Moses Johnson the sum of fifty dollars each the amount of their several recognisance in this behalf acknowledged unless sufficient cause for such failure be shewn -
    And Court adjourned untill tomorrow morning 9 O'clock
                                    Hugh D. Hale
                                    Joseph Brown
                                    M. Lincoln
    Saturday 29th. July 1826 Court met present

    The Minutes of yesterdays proceedings were read and signed

Mary Ann Donnekin)
    vs.)   Motion for Allowance the maintenance
Joshua Bowling, Junr.)   of a Bastard Child

    The plaintiff by her attorney, James P. Taylor esquire moved the Court here for judgment against the Defendant and Security for an allowance for the maintenance of a Bastard (P-129) child begoten of the body of Mary Ann Donnekin of this County single woman for one year from the present. Upon consideration whereof it is ordered by the court that the Plaintiff be allowed the sum of forty dollars for the maintainance of said child for one year from the present court and that the saidDefendant and Joshua Bowling Senr. pay the aforesaid allowance at the costs of this motion.

John Love   )
   vs   )   Certio. Rule to dismiss
George Welty)

        The plaintiff by Attorney discharges the rule heretofore entered to shew cause why the Defendants petition and writ should be dismissed -

William McDannel)
   vs   )   Covenant. Demurrer to Declaration -
Jacob Newman   )

        This day came the parties by Attornies and thereupon the Defendants Demurrer to the plaintiffs Declaration came on for argument - Whereupon all and singular the premises being seen and by the court fully understood - It is considered that said Demurrer be overruled and that the plaintiff recover against the Defendant his damages by occasion in the Declaration mentioned but because it is unknown to the Court what those Damages are. It is ordered that a jury come here at the next court to enquire of Damages between the parties in this suit.

(P-130)
Lewis Ball   )
   vs.   )   Cont. Demurrer to Declaration
James Allen   )
& Conrad Girdner)   This day came the parties by attornies
                  and the thereupon the Defendants Demurrer to the Declaration of the plaintiff came on for argument. Whereupon all and singular the premises being seen and by the Court fully understood. It is considered that the Defendants Demurrer be sustained - and on motion of the plaintiff by attorney he is permited to amend the Declaration in this suit on payment of the costs of the amendment.

Isaac Baker   )
   vs   )   Certio
Jacob Rimal   )

        From the judgment rendered at the present Term of this Court the plaintiff by Attorney prays an appeal to the next Circuit Court of Law to be held for the County of Greene in the Courthouse in Greenville on the firs t Monday in September next and having given bond and security to prosecute his appeal is granted and the proceedings ordered to be certified.

Nathan Hawkins)
   vs   )   Certio. Rule to dismiss
William Britton)

This day came the parties by Attornies and thereupon
the Rule entered to shew cause why the Defendants petition
and writ should be dismissed came on for argument. Whereupon all(P-131) and singular the premises being seen and by
the Court fully understood. It is considered that said rule
be made absolute and that the plaintiff recover against the
Defendant and Elijah Kidwell Security for the prosecution of
his writ of certiorari the sum of eight dollars and sixty one
cents with interest thereon from the 22nd day of April one
thousand eight hundred and twenty six and his costs of him
about his suit in this behalf expended.

Johnson Frazier for the)
  use of Thomas Frasier)
     vs)   Certio. Rule to Quash
Isaac Walker)

    This day came the parties by attor-
nies and thereupon the Rule entered to shew cause why the proceedings before the justice of the peace should be quashed
came on for argument. Whereupon all and singular the premises
being seen and by the Court fully understood. It is considered
that said rule be made absolute - that the proceedings before
the justice of the peace in this cause be quashed and that the
Defendant recover against Thomas Frasier for whose use this
Suit was brought his costs by him about his Defence in this
behalf expended -

Samuel Leming)
    vs)   Covenant -
James Bailey)

    This day came the plaintiff by by Attorney
and the Defendant although solemnly called came not but made
default (P-132) Therefore it is considered that the plaintiff recover against the Defendant his Damages by occasion in
the Declaration mentioned but because it is unknown to the
Court what those damages are. It is ordered that a jury come
here at the next court to enquire of Damages between the parties in this suit -

Mordecai Lincoln)
    vs) Ca. Sa. Issued by Keeper of Justices
Christopher Cook &)   Records
John Walker Secy.)

    The Defendant having been arrested
by virtue of a Ca. Sa. issued by Alexander Brown keeper of
Justices Records for this County at the Suit of the plaintiff
for the sum of three dollars forty six and three fourth cents
debt and the further sum of one dollar eighty seven ½ cents
for costs - and having entered into bond with John Walker,
Security for his personal appearance here at the present Court
to surrender property in discharge of said debt or to take
the benefit of the insolvent debtors oath and having failed to
comply with said bond - Therefore on motion of the plaintiff
by John A. Aiken, his Attorney. It is considered that the
plaintiff recover against the said Defendant and John Walker

The Defendant having been arrested by virtue of a ca. sa. issued by Mordecai Lincoln esquire an acting justice of the peace for this County at the suit of the plaintiff for the sum of one dollar and seventy cents debt and one dollar cost and having entered into bond with James Thomson, Security for his appearance here at the present court to surrender property in discharge of said Debt or to take the benefit of the insolvent debtors oath, and having failed to comply with said bond on motion of the plaintiff by John A. Aiken, his Attorney. It is considered that the plaintiff (P-135) recover against the said Defendant and James Thomson his Security the said Sum of one Dollar and Seventy cents debt with the further sum of one dollar cost and the cost of this motion -

John Guin   )
   vs.   )   Ca. Sa. Issued by Keeper of
Samuel R. Gauntt and   )   Justices Records.
James Thompson, Security)

                    The Defendant having been arrested by virtue of a Ca. Sa. issued by Alexander Brown keeper of justices Records of this County at the suit of the plaintiff for the sum of Twenty dollars and eighty five cents debt and one dollar and twenty five cents costs - and having entered into bond with James Thomson Security for his appearance here at the present court to surrender property in discharge of sd, Debt or to take the benefit of the insolvent debtors oath and having failed to comply with said bond - On motion of the plaintiff by John A. Aiken his Attorney- It is considered that he recover against the said Samuel K. Gauntt and James Thompson, his Security the aforesaid sum of twenty dollars and eighty five cents debt with interest thereon at the rate of 6 pr centum pr. annum from the 21st. day of August 1824 with the sum of one dollar and Twenty five cents costs and the costs of this motion -

Valentine Sevier, surviving   )
  partner of Deaderick &   )   Ca. Sa. Issued by a
  Sevier for David A. Deaderick)   Justice of the peace
     VS.   )
James McAmis and Samuel McAmis)

                    The Defendant having been arrested by virtue of a Ca. Sa. issued by Richard West esq. (P-136) an acting justice of the peace for said county at the suit of the plaintiff, for the sum of thirty nine dollars and fifty three cents debt and one dollar costs and having entered into bond with Samuel McAmis, security for his appearance here at the present Court to surrender property in discharge of said Debtor to take the benefit of the insolvent Debtors oath and having failed to comply with said Bond on motion of the plaintiff by John A. Aiken his Attorney it is considered that the plaintiff recover against the said Defendant and Samuel McAmis his security the aforesaid sum of thirty nine Dollars and fifty three cents with interest thereon at the rate of 6 per continue per annum from the 6th. day of

August 1825 with the further sum of one dollar for costs
and also the costs of the motion -

John Kennedy)
vs) Whereas it appears that on the 20th
Michael Dyche Admr.) day of May 1826 the plaintiff recov-
of Henry Dyche, Decd.) - ered a judgment against the Defendant and Henry Dyche esquire for the
sum of forty dollars and forty four cents debt and one dollar
cost before Mordecas Lincoln, esquire an acting justice of the
peace for said County on which judgment on execution appears
to have issued and which is not returned by Richard M. Woods
Sheriff of Greene County no personal property found and the
papers being returned by the justice aforesaid on the applica-
tion of the plaintiff and it being now suggested to the Court
(P-137) that the said Henry Dyche Sen. died sued and possessed of real estate within the County of Greene which decended
to Henry Dyche, Michael Dyche, Christain Dyche, John Dyche,
William H. Moore, and Catherine his wife formerly Catherine
Dyche, Nathaniel D. Moore and Peggy his wife formerly Peggy
Dyche, Elizabeth Dyche, and Christiana Dyche heirs of Henry
Dyche dec. Whereupon on motion of the plaintiff by Seth I.
O. Luckey, his attorney Scire Facia is awarded him against
the aforesaid heirs commanding them to appear at our next
Court of Pleas and Quarter Sessions to be held for the County
of Greene in the Courthouse in Greeneville on the fourth
Monday in October next to shew cause if any they can why the
plaintiff this execution for the amount of his judgment and
costs aforesaid of the lands and tenement of which the said
Henry Dyche decd died seized and possessed ought not to have
according to the act of assembly in such case made and provided

State of Tennessee)
and Peter Sellers) Surety of the peace required
vs.)
David Millburn Junr.) William Milburn acknowledged to owe
the State of Tennessee the Sum of
fifty dollars yet upon conditions that if David Milburn Junr
a minor shall keep the peace toward all the good people of the
State of Tennessee for six months from the present time but
especially towards Peter Sellers then the above recogniance
to be void otherwise in force - whereupon it is ordered that
the said David Milburn Junr. pay the costs in this behalf expended - (P-138)

State of Tennessee)
and Thomas Harvey) Certio Rule to Dismiss
vs.)
John Thomason) This day came the parties by attornies and thereupon the rule entered
to shew cause why the Defendants petition and writ should be
dismissed came on for argument whereupon all and singular the
premeses being seen and by the court fully understood - It
is considered that said rule be discharged and that this suit
be continued for Trial -

For Satisfactory reasons appearing to the Court ordered
that the Clerk issue execution in all cases against those
Defendants where a connection has taken place and in which
the costs have been ordered to be paid by the Trustee of
Greene County- where there may be a probality of the costs
being collected from the said Defendants -

And Court adjourned until court in course until which
time all matters and things in the same depending and unde-
ermed acct. continued.

Jesse Kerby
M. Lincoln

(P-139)
State of Tennessee

At a Court of Pleas and Quarter Sessions continued and
held for the County of Greene in the Courthouse in Greeneville
on the Fourth Monday being the 23rd. day of October one thous-
and eight hundred and twenty six- was present

George Robertson)
   vs.   )   T.V.A.
Thomas Collier)

The plaintiff in his proper person appeared
in court and dismissed his suit and considered that the plaintiff recover against the Defendant his costs by him about his
suit in this behalf expended -

State of Tennessee)
   vs   )   Bastardy
Cross Scruggs)

Margaret Shannon in her proper person
appeared in court and assumed for and on behalf of the Defendant the payment of the fine and costs of this prosecution and
agrees that judgment be entered against her for the same
Therefore it is considered that the State of Tennessee recover
against the said Margaret Shannon the fine and costs aforesaid
according to her assumpsit -

State of Tennessee)
   vs   )   Sci Fa. Forfeiture Recogn.
Cross Scruggs)

On motion ordered that the forfeiture
in this writ of Scire Facias named to set aside on payment
out of the costs thereof by the (P-140) Defendant who being
present in Court assumes the payment of the same- and thereupon Margaret Shannon appeared in court in her proper person
and assumed for and on behalf of the Defendant the payment
of the cost aforesaid and agrees that judgment be entered
against her for the same. Therefore it is considered that
the State of Tennessee recover against the said Margaret
Shannon the costs aforesaid according to her assumpsit.

State and Edith Woods)
   vs.   ) Bastardy
Cross Scruggs)

Edith Woods in her proper person appeared in Court & acknowledges to have received of Gross Scruggs full satisfaction of all claims against him in consequence of his being counted as being the father a Bastard child begoten of her body by the said Gross Scruggs and Court adjourned untill tomorrow morning 9 o'clock.

Joseph Brown
John Matthews
Thos. Smith

(P-141)   Tuesday 24th. Octr. 1826
      Court met present.

The Minutes of yesterday proceedings were read & signed-

John Love   )
   vs   )   Certio. Continued by consent.
George Welty   )

John Matthews, assignee)
   John Noncaster   ))   Appeal
   vs   )
George Bell, Applt   )   On motion and cause shewn by
                             affidavit, John Matthews this
cause is continued untill next court.

Jacob T. Wyrick)
   vs.   )   Certio
Andrew Park   )
                 Continued as on affidavit of Defendant.

Zachariah Kinnoman)
   vs   )   Debt
Hugh Broadrick   )
                 By consent of the parties this cause is
transfered to the Circuit Court of Greene County for Trial &
the Clerk of this Court is directed to make out an extract
and bill of costs of said suit.

(P-142)   Tuesday 24th. Octr. 1826
Hannah Baker)
   vs.   )   Certio
Isaac Baker)
                 On motion ordered that this suit be revived
in the name of Daniel Allen executor of Hannah Baker Decd. -

George Bell   )
   vs.   ) Certio
Henry A. Farnsworth)
                 Continued as on affidavit plaintiff.

John Baker   )
   vs   )   Certio
Howell Houston and   )
William Houston   )

Continued as on affidavit William Houston - and on motion ordered that the order made at last court for taking testimony in this cause be revived -

William McDannel)
 vs   ) Debt
Jacob Newman)

  On motion and cause shewn by affidavit of Defendant this cause is continued untill next court -

  Richard M. Woods, esquire High Sheriff in and for the County of Greene returns here into open court the States writ of Venire Facias to him directed endorsed returnable Tuesday after the fourth Monday in October - Issd. 14th. August 1826 executed on all but Stephen Manes, Anthony Bewley, Robert Lester, R. M. Woods, Sheriff " Out of whom are selected as the (P.143.) Tuesday 24th. October 1826. Statutes in that case provides the following person as Grand Inquest and jury to wit
James Park appointed foreman of the Court

James Matthews	Chrisley Bible
William Matthews	John McMackin
Matthew Cox	Jacob Sailor
Henry Bible	Samuel Bowman
Peter Fry	Philip Harman
Jacob Bird	Barnabas G. Myers

good and lawful men of the County of Greene who being now here empanneled and sworn to esquire for the State aforesaid and for the Body of the County of Greene received their charge and retired from the Bar -

  James Gass, a constable was qualified to attend on the above jury 3 days -- Certificate -

  On motion and for satisfactory reasons appearing to the court ordered that William D. Neilson, Alexander Brown and Silas Dobson be released from further attendance at the present court as jurors --

  John Kennedy, Robert Leming, James Lowry, Benjamin Brotherton, George Frazier, Abraham Brown and Thomas Justis the residue of the Venire to the present Court are to attend the same as pettit jurors respectively untill discharged --

  Jacob Bible to attend as a constable on the Court 4 days
      4 days certificate issd.

(P-144) Tuesday 24th. Octr. 1826
Thomas Stroud)
 vs.   ) Certio
William Boling)
  This day came the parties by Attornies and thereupon a jury to wit John Kennedy, Robert Leming, Thomas Justis, John Baker, Chrisley Harmon, George Bell, John Thomason, Samuel Mitchell, Moses Harmon, Samuel Walker, Henry

Long, William McDannel who being elected tried sworn well
and truly to try this cause upon their oath do say that they
find for the plaintiff forty eight dollars and twenty five
cents. Therefore it is considered that the plaintiff recover
against the Defendant and Joshua Boling security for the
prosecution of his writ of certiorari the aforesaid sum of
forty eight dollars and twenty five cents and his costs by
him about his suit in this behalf expended -

William McDannel)
   vs   )   Covenant -
Jacob Newman   )

                  The Plaintiff dismisses his suit and assumes
the payment of five dollars of the costs of this suit and the
defendant assumes the payment of the remaining costs. Therefore it is considered that the parties recover against each
other the costs aforesaid according to their assumpsit.

Barbara Kirk for herself and)
as Guardian of the minor   )   Petition continued
heirs of Joseph Kirk decd.)
     vs.   )
Joseph Davis   )

(P-145) Tuesday 24th. Octr. 1826
Samuel Leming   )
assignee Stephen Johnson   )   Covt
   vs   )
John Click & Martin Click   )   This day came the parties
                                      by attorneys and there-
upon a jury to wit James Lowry, Benjamin Brotherton, Peter
Whittenberg, William Mitchell, Joseph Brodley, Peter Swatrel
John Gass, (of John) Samuel McAmish, John McCollum, John Gass
(of James) Patrick Coggburn and James Lackland who being elected tried and sworn the truth to speak upon the issue joined
upon their oath do say that the Defendant have not kept and
performed their covenant as in pleading they have alleged but
have broken the same in manner and form as the plaintiff against them in his declaration hath complained and they do assess
the plaintiffs damages by occasion thereof to one hundred and
seven dollars and thirty nine cents- Therefore it is considered that the Plaintiff recover against the Defendant the Damages
by the jury aforesaid assessed and his costs by him about his
suit in this behalf expended -

Daniel M. Guin   )
   vs.   ) Appeal
Ephraim Wilson Exr.   )
of Robert Wilson Decd. Applt) Continued on affidavit defendant

(P-146)   Tuesday Octr. 1826.

Boyd McNairy)
  vs.   ) Debt
Alexander Sevier)

    This day came the parties by attornies
and thereupon a jury to wit John Kennedy, Robert Leming,
Thomas Justis, John Baker, Chrisley Harmon, George Bell,
John Thomason, Samuel Mitchell, Moses Harmon, Samuel Walker
Henry Long and William McDannel, who being elected tried and
sworn well and truly to try this cause upon their oath do
say that the writing obligatory mentioned in the plaintiffs
declaration was not executed to secure the said sum of money
for so much won by the plaintiff off the Defendant at a game
of Haeard or address called Bragg at the plaintiff by by
replying hath alledged - and they do assess the plaintiffs
Damages by occasion thereof to thirty one dollars and eighty
cents - Therefore it is considered that the plaintiff recover
against the Defendant the sum of one hundred and seventy
dollars the debt in the declaration mentioned with the Damages
by the jury aforesaid assessed and his costs by him about his
suit in this behalf expended -

James Scruggs & Co.)
  vs.   ) Debt
George Gordan)

    This day came the plaintiff by attorney
and the Defendant although solemnly called came not but made
default - Therefore it is considered by the court that the
plaintiffs recover against the Defendant the sum of four hundred and three dollars eighty three and one half cents (P-147)
the Debt inthe Declaration mentioned with the further sum of
sixty eight Dollars and forty five cents for Interest due
and accrued up to the present time and his costs by him about
his suit in this behalf expended -

John Blanton)
 vs   ) Certio
John Ross)

    This day came the parties by attornies and
thereupon a jury to wit James Lowery, Benjamin Brotherton
Peter Whittenburg, William Mitchell, Joseph Bradley, Peter
Swatrel, John Gass , (of John) Samuel McAmish, John McCollum
John Gass (of James) Patrick Coggurn and James Lockland,
who being elected tried and sworn well and truly to try this
cause upon their oath do say that they find for the Defendant
Therefore it is considered that the plaintiff take nothing as
his Suit and that the Defendant recover against the plaintiff
his cost by him about his Defence in this behalf expended -

Jonathan Harrold)
 vs   ) Appeal
William Roberts Applt)

      This day came the parties by attornies
      and thereupon a jury to wit George
Frazier, Abraham Brown, William Gass, Nathan Hawkins, John

Wright, John Brotherton, Smith Harvey, Absalom Thompson, Jeremiah Casteel, James McClelland who being elected tried and sworn well and truly to try this cause upon their oath do say thatthey find for the plaintiff two dollars - There upon it is considered that (P-148) the plaintiff recover against the Defendant and John Roberts Security for the prosecution of his appeal the aforesaid sum of Two Dollars and his costs by him about his suit in this behalf expended -

State of Tennessee)
Samuel McKeehan, Pros.)   Pettit Larceny
        vs)
John Brown)   The Defendant acknowledged to
                    owe the State of Tennessee the
sum of one hundred dollars and John Lauderdale and James Gibson his sureties acknowledge to owe the State of Tennessee the sum of twenty five dollars each yet upon condition that John Brown shall make his personal appearance from day to day of the present court and answer the State of Tennessee of Tennessee of a a charge against him for the commission of Pettit Larceny and not depart the court without cause then the above recogniances to be void otherwise in force -

Marion Tilford and Ebeneser)
Matthews Executrix and)   Debt Speecle -
Executor of Thomas Tilford Decd.)
        vs.)   The Defendant by attorney
                    with drawing the plea of
John Snapp)   payment confesses that he
asses the plaintiffs the sum of Two hundred thirteen dollars ninety eight cents. Therefore it is considered that the plaintiff recover against the Defendant the aforesaid two hundred thirteen dollars and ninety eight cents sum of and the costs by them about their suit in this behalf expended - (P-149)

        Tuesday 24th. Octr. 1826
William Senter and)
Thomas Hale executors of)   The Defendants in their
Nehemiah Pettit, decd.)   proper person came into
        vs.)   court and confess judg-
Valentine Ketring, Jacob Kinsor)   ment according to Specialty
Adam Ketring and Henry Fry)   Therefore it is considered
and Adam Ketring of Adam)   that the plaintiff recover
Ketring decd.)   against the Defendant
                    Valentine Ketring, Jacob
Kinsor and Adam Ketring Junr. the sum of three hundred dollars the debt in the specialty mentioned with the further sum of thirty five dollars and seventy fivecents for interest due and accused thereon and their costs by them about their suit in this behalf expended - and it is admitted that Henry Fry hath fully administrated all and singular the goods and chattels of Adam Ketring decd. except the sum of one hundred and forty dollars for which he has confessed judgment in another of these suits therefore let the said Henry Fry go hence without day in this suit   execution stand 6 Months.

Same)
  vs.)   Debt
Same)

     The Defendants Valentine Ketring, Jacob Kinsor and Adam Ketring and confees that they owe the plaintiffs' the sum of two hundred fifty dollars the residue of the specialty on which this suit was brought together with the further sum of forty eight dollars for interest due and accrued thereon and the Defendant Henry Fry confesses that he has in his hands of the goods and chattels of Adam Ketring decd. the sum of one hundred and forty dollars for which he confesses judgment It is thereupon considered that the plaintiffs recover against the Defendants Valentine Ketring, Jacob Kinsor and Adam Ketring the sum of Two (P-150) hundred and fifty dollars with the further sum of forty eight dollars for the interest due and accrued thereon and also that he recover of Henry Fry the aforesaid sum of one hundred and forty dollars for which he hath confessed to have in his hands assests of the estate of Adam Ketring Senr. decd. but that the plaintiffs are not to collect off of all or any of the Defendants more than the sum of Two hundred and ninety eight dollars and that the plaintiff recover against the defendants their costs by them about their suit in this behalf expended -

     execution stand 6 months

Same)
  vs)   Debt
Same)

     The Defendants Valentine Ketring, Jacob Kinsor and Adam Ketring confesses that they owe the plaintiff the sum of two hundred and fifty dollars the amount of the specialty decd and. on with the further sum of seventy five dollars for interest due accrued thereon - Therefore it is considered that the plaintiffs recover against the said Defendants Valentine Ketring, Jacob Kinsor, and Adam Ketring the aforesaid sum of two hundred and fifty dollars according to their confession with the further sum of seventy five dollars for interest due and accrued thereon and their costs by them about their suit in this behalf expended -
     And that Henry Fry one of the Defendants in this suit go hence without day
     execution stand 6 months

(P-151)   Tuesday 24th. 1826.

Same)
  vs.)   Debt
Same)

     The defendants Valentine Ketring, Jacob Kinsor and Adam Ketring confess that they owe the plaintiff the sum of Two hundred and fifty dollars the amount of the specialty declared on with the further sum of sixty dollars for interest due and accrued thereon- Therefore it is considered

that the plaintiff recover against the said Valentine Ketring
Jacob Kinsor and Adam Ketring the aforesaid sum of two hundred and fifty dollars according to their confession with the
further sum of Sixty Dollars for interest due and accrued
thereon - Therefore it is considered that the plaintiff recover
against the said Valentine Ketring, Jacob Kinsor, and Adam
Ketring the aforesaid sum of Two hundred and fifty dollars
according to their confession with the further sum of sixty
dollars for the interest due and accrued thereon and their
costs by them about their suit in this behalf expended -
And that Henry Fry one of the Defendants in this suit
go hence without day -

execution Staid 6 months
And Court adjourned untill tomorrow morning 9 o'clock.

John Matthes
Thos. Smith
Lewis Ball

(P-152)   Wednesday 25th. Octr. 1826
            Court met present

The Minutes of yesterdays proceedings were read and signed

Robert Patterson)
    vs.   ) Certio
David E. W. Bable &)
Jacob Newman   ) On motion of plaintiff by attorney
                    a rule is allowed him to shew cause
who the defendants petition and writ should be dismissed and
the plaintiff by attorney files the cross affidavit of Leonard
Starnes in this suit -

State of Tennessee)
Bryant Deaton, prosr.)
vs.   ) T. A. B.
James Johnson   )
                    Continued - James Johnson acknowledged
to owe the State of Tennessee one hundred dollars and Tilman
A. Howard his surety also acknowledged to owe the State of
Tennessee fifty dollars yet upon condition that if James Johnson shall make his personal appearances at the Court of pleas
and quarter sessions to be held for the county of Greene in
the Courthouse in Greeneville on Wednesday next after the
fourth Monday in January next and stand his trial in this
prosecution against him and not depart the court without leave
then the above recognizance to be void otherwise in force.
(P-153)
        Wednesday 25th. October 1826
Bryant Decaton, Prosr.)
    vs.   ) T. A. B.
Peter Brown   )
                    Continued as on affidavit prosecutor
Peter Brown acknowledged to owe the State of Tennessee one
hundred and Tilman H. Howard esquire his surety also acknowledge to owe the State of Tennessee fifty dollars yet upon

condition that if Peter Brown shall make his personal appearance at the Court of Pleas and Quarter Session to be held for the County of Greene in the Courthouse in Greeneville on Wednesday next after the fourth Monday in January next and stand his trial in this prosecution against him and not depart the court without leave then this recognizance to be void otherwise in force -

John Robertson for Samuel)
Caldwell's use)   Covenant
    vs.)
James Tadlock and Thomas Caldwell) Demurrer to Declaration

This day came the parties by Attornies and thereupon the Defendants demurrer to the plaintiffs declaration came on for argument- Whereupon all and singular the premise being seen and by occasion in the declaration mentioned. But because it is unknown to the Court what those damages are - It is ordered that a jury come here at the next term of this court to enquire of Damages between the parties in this Suit   (P-154)

    Wednesday 25th. Octr. 1826
Samuel Leming, Assignee)
  Stephen Johnson)   Covenant
    vs.)
James Bailey)   This day came the plaintiff by

Attorney and thereupon a jury to wit George Frazier, Benjamin Brotherton, Thomas Batt, John Brotherton, Patrick Coggburn, William Barkley, Joseph Henry, Daniel Reeser, James Jack, James McKeehan, Thomas Harvey, Peter Swatrel, who being elected tried and sworn well and truly toenquire of Damages between the parties upon their oath do say that the plaintiff has sustained Damages by occasion in the declaration mentioned to the amount of fifty nine dollars - Therefore it is considered that the plaintiff recover against the Defendant the Damages aforesaid by the jury aforesaid assessed and his costs by him about his suit in this behalf expended -

State of Tennessee &)
  Thomas Harvey)   Certiorari
    vs.)
John Thomason)   This day came the parties by attornies and thereupon a jury to wit George Frazier, Benjamin Brotherton, Thomas Batt, John Brotherton, Patrick Coggburn, William Barkly, Joseph Henry, Daniel Reeser, James Jack, James McKeehan, Thomas Lawson, and Jeremiah Jack who being elected tried and sworn well and truly to try this cause upon their oath do say that they find for the defendant Therefore it is considered that the Defendant go hence and recover against Thomas   (P-155) Harvey his costs by him about his suit in this behalf expended

Wyly Craft)
    vs.)   Certio
Jotham Brown, Jr.)

A Commission is awarded the defendant to take deposition of Alexander Dugger of Roane County which may be directed to any one justice of the peace of this County by giving the plaintiff twenty four hours notice of the time and place of executing such commission

Isaac Baker)
vs.) Motion for Judgment for monies paid by
William Dunn) plaintiff as security for Defendant.

It appearing to the satisfaction of the Court that the plaintiff was security for the Defendant that in consequence of becoming security as aforesaid he has been compelled to pay the sum of fifty four dollars and fifty four cents - (P-156) Therefore on motion of the plaintiff by James Wyly his attorney it is considered that he recover against the Defendant the aforesaid sum of fifty four dollars and fifty four cents and the costs of this motion

State of Tennessee)
Jno. Cummings Prosr.) Assault offend to Nancy Cummings
vs.)
John Rymal) The Defendant who stands bound by
recognizance in the sum of one hundred dollars for his appearance here was solemnly called for that purpose but came not: Therefore it is considered that the State of Tennessee recover against the said John Rymal the sum of one hundred dollars the amount of his recognizance in this behalf acknowledged unless sufficient cause for such failure be shown and thereupon Levi Dann and John Guinn who stand bound by recognizance in the sum of fifty dollars for the appearance here of John Rymal were severally solemnly called to bring into court the body of the said John Rymal and surrender the same in discharge of themself as bail but failed so to do and made default. Therefore it is considered that the State of Tennessee recover against the said Levi Dunn and John Guinn the sum of fifty dollars each unless sufficient cause be shewn -

State of Tennessee)
John Cummings, Prosr.) T. A. B.
vs.)
John Rymal) The Defendant who stands bound by
recognizance in the sum of one hundred (P-157) Dollars for his appearance here was solemnly called for that purpose but came not. Therefore it is considered that the State of Tennessee recover against the said John Rymal the sum of one hundred dollars the amount of one hundred dollars the amount of his recognizance in this behalf acknowledged unless sufficient cause for such failure be shewn - and thereupon Levi Dunn and John Guinn who stand bound by recognizance in the sum of fifty dollars for the appearance here of John Rymal were severally solemnly called to being into court the body of the said John Rymal and surrender the same in discharge of themselves as bail but failed so to do and made default. Therefore it is

considered that the State of Tennessee recover against the said Levi Dunn and John Guinn the sum of fifty dollars each unless sufficient cause shall be shewn -

James Mc.Pherron)
   vs.) Certio
James Gibson)

     On motion of plaintiff by attorney a rule is allowed him to shew cause why the defendants petition and writ should be dismissed.

State of Tennessee)
  Samuel McKahan, Prosr.) Indict for Pettit Larceny
  vs.)
John Brown) The Grand Jury having returned
                           not a true bill it is ordered thatthe Defendant be discharged from his recognizance .

(P-158)   Wednesday 25th. October 1826.

State of Tennessee)
  Amos Garrett, Prosr.) T. A. B.
  VS.)
George Freshour) This day came as well the Attorney General as the Defendant in his proper person and the Defendant in his proper person and the defendant being charged on the Bill of Indictment for plea says that he is not guilty in manner and form as therein against him is alledged and puts himself on the Country and the Attorney General having done the same came also a jury to wit Abraham Brown, James Lowery Thomas Hays John Baker, Samuel Gass, William Lawson, Peter Swatrel, Thomas Harvey, John Thomason, Jesse Morgan, Bryant Deaton who being elected tried and sworn the truth to speak upon this issue of Traverse upon their oath do say that the Defendant is guilty in manner and form as charged in the Bill of Indictment.

    Therefore it is considered that the Defendant for such his offence be fined forfeit and pay to the State of Tennessee the sum of one dollar and that he pay the costs of this prosecution and thereupon came William Houston and assumed for and on behalf of the defendant the payment of the fine and costs aforesaid and agrees that judgment be entered against him for the same -

    Therefore it is considered that the State of Tennessee recover against the said William Houston the fine and costs aforesaid according to his assumpsit

(P-159)   Wednesday 25th. Octr. 1826

Amos Garrett, Prosr.)
   vs.) Assault
Martin Cleve)

    This day came as well the Attorney General as the Defendant being charged on the bill of Indictment for plea says that he is not guilty in manner and form as therein against him is alledged and puts himself on the

County and the Attorney General having done the same came also a jury to wit, John Kennedy, Robert Leming, Thomas Justis, Seburn Jewell, Elias Carton, Thomas Oliphant Thomas Davis, David Hartley, Joseph McCurry, John Bettner, Samuel Gass, and John Casteel who being elected tried and sworn the truth to speak upon this issue of Traverse upon their oath do say that the Defendant is guilty in manner and form as charged in the Bill of Indictment. Therefore it is considered that the Defendant for such his offence be fined forfeit and pay to the State of Tennessee the sum of one dollar and that he pay the costs of this prosecution - and thereupon came Andrew Stephens Junr. and assumed the payment of thefine and costs aforesaid and agrees that judgment be entered against him for the same -

Therefore it is considered that the State of Tennessee recover against the said Andrew Stephens Junr. and assumed for and on behalf of Defendant the payment of the fine and costs aforesaid and agrees that judgment be entered against him for the same-

Therefore it is considered that the State of Tennessee recover against the said Andrew Stephens Junr. the fine and costs aforesaid according to his assumpsit -

(P-160) Wednesday 25th. Octr. 1826.

Ordered that Hamell Houston and Andrew Stephens Junr. for a breach of the peace commited within the range of the court enter into recognizance to answer the same.

Whereupon Howell Houston acknowledged to owe to the State of Tennessee one hundred dollars and James Bailey his Surety also acknowledged to owe to the State of Tennessee fifty dollars - yet upon condition that if Howell Houston shall make his personal appearance from day to day during the present term of this court and answer the foregoing charge then the above recognizance to be void otherwise in force -

Andrew Stephens also acknowledged to owe the State of Tennessee one hundred dollars and Thomas Jackson his surety also acknowledged to owe to the State of Tennessee fifty dollars - Yet upon condition that if Andrew Stephens shall make his personal appearance from day to day during the present term of this court and answer the foregoing charge then the above recognizance to be void otherwise in force -

State of Tennessee)
 Moses Johnson, Prosr.) Assault
  vs.   )
James Long   ) This day came as well the attorney
            general as the Defendant in his
proper person and the Defendant in his proper person and the Defendant being charged in the Bill of Indictment for plea thereto says that he is not guilty in manner and form (P-161) as therein against him is alleged and puts himself on the Country and the Attorney General having done the same came also a jury to wit George Frazier, Benjamin Brotherton

Thomas Batt, John Brotherton, Patrick Coggburn, Joseph
Henry, James Bailey, James McMahan, Jeremiah Jack, Thomas
Lawson, John Hoyal, Daniel McLain, who being elected tried
and sworn the truth to speak upon this issue of traverse
upon their oath do say that the Defendant is guilty in
manner and form as charged in the Bill of Indictment -
Therefore it is considered that the Defendant for such his
offence be find forfeit and pay to the State of Tennessee,
the sum of one dollar and that he pay the costs of this
prosecution - And thereupon came Reubin Long and Jesse
Morgan, and assumed for and on behalf of the defendant the
payment of the fine and costs aforesaid and agree that
judgment be entered against them for the same - Therefore
it is considered that the State of Tennessee recover against
the said Reubin Long and Jesse Morgan the fine and costs
aforesaid according to their assumpsit

     Thomas Justis, a juror is released from further attend-
ance at this court.

Isaac Humbard   )
   vs.   ) Certio
James Hise   )
                  The petition of the Defendant was presented
by Tilman A. Howard esquire his attorney praying writs of
certiorari and   (P-162) Sa persedeas. Upon consideration
whereof It is ordered that writs issued pursant to the
prayer of said petition on Bond and Security being given
according to law.

John Matthews, assignee)
John Mooncaster   ) Appeal
   vs.   )
George Bell   ) The plaintiff in his proper person
                     appeared in court and dismissed his
suit and assumes the costs -
     Therefore it is considered that the plaintiff take nothing
by his suit and that the Defendant recover against the plaintiff and Ira Greene his Security his costs by him about his
defence in this behalf expended -

(P-163)   Wednesday 25th. Octr. 1826
Hugh Malony   )
   vs.   ) Ca. Sa. Issued by a Justices
Christian Dyche and   )   of the Peace filed 24th
William S. Perry, Security)   October 24th. 1826.
                  The Defendant having been
arrested by virtue of a Ca. Sa. issued by Joseph Brown esquire
an acting justice of the peace for the County at the suit
of the plaintiff for the sum of Twenty four dollars and forty
six cents debt and the cost and having entered intered into
Bond with William S. Perry Security for the appearance here
at the present court to comply with the late law respecting
insolvent Debtors being liberated from custody order a Ca. Sa.
and having failed to comply with the aforesaid Bond - But on

yesterday having filed a schedule of his property on oath -
Therefore on motion of the plaintiff by James W. Wyly
his attorney It is considered by the court that the plaintiff
recover against the said Defendant and William S. Perry his
Security the aforesaid sum of twenty four dollars and forty
six cent with interest thereon at the rate of six per centum.
pr. annum from the 11th. day of March last and the costs and
also the costs of this motion -

(P-164)   Wednesday 25th. Octr. 1826
Lewis Ball   )
    vs.   ) Covenant
James Allen & Girdner) Demurrer to Declaration as amanded -
                             This day came the parties by
attornies and thereupon the Defendants demurrer, to the amended
declaration of the plaintiff came on for argument - Whereupon
Counsel being heard and all and singular the premesis being
seen and by the Court fully understood - It is considered
that the declaration of the plaintiff and the matters and
things therein continued on not good and sufficient in law
to enable the plaintiff his action against the said Defendants
to have and maintain. Therefore it is considered that the
plaintiff take nothing by his suit and that the plaintiff
their costs by them about their suit in this behalf expended -

State of Tennessee   )
    vs.   )   Bastardy
Drusella B. Hutchison)
                      The Defendant who stands bound by
recognizance for her appearance here to indemify the County
of Greene from all charges in consequence of the birth and
maintenance of a Bastard child of which she refuses to declare
the father appeared accordingly and entered into bond in the
sum of five hundred with George Henderson on security condition
that the said Drusella B. Hutchison shall perform such order
as the court shall from time to time make concerning (P-165)
the maintainance of said child- Whereupon it is ordered that
the Defendant pay the costs in this behalf expended - and
thereupon George Anderson assumed for the Defendant the payment of the costs aforesaid and agrees that judgment be entered
against him for the same -
Therefore it is considered that the State of Tennessee
recover against the said George Henderson the costs aforesaid
according to his assumpsit -
And Court adjourned until tomorrow morning 9 o'clock
                              M. Lincoln, J.P.
                              John Matthews
                              Leonard Stoner

Thursday 26th. Octr. 1826 Court met present

The Minutes of yesterdays proceedings were read and signed-

John Balch)
  vs.   )   Case
John Blair)

        The plaintiff dismisses his suit and the defendant assumes the costs - Therefore it is considered that the plaintiff recover against the defendant his costs by him about his suit in this behalf expended - and T. A. Howard releases his Tax Fee -

(P-166)   Thursday 26th. Octr. 1826   )
James H. Alexander, Administrator of)   The defendant with
Alexander Decd.   ) drawing the plea here-
   vs.   )tofore filed - and con-
John Blair   )fesses that he owes the
                              plaintiff the sum of
                            fifty dollars the Residue
of the Debt in the Declaration mentioned - Therefore it is considered that the plaintiff recover against the Defendant the aforesaid and his costs by him about his suit in this behalf expended -

Lewis Ball   )
  vs.   )   Covt.
James Allen and)
Conrad Girdner) From the judgment rendered in this cause at
                   the present term of this court the plaintiff by Attorney prays an appeal to the next circuit of Greene County to be held in the Courthouse in Greeneville on the first Monday in March next and having given bond and security to prosecute - his appeal is granted and the proceedings ordered to be certified

William Wilson   )
  vs.   )   Sci Fa.
The Heirs at Law and   )
Children of John Russell decd.)   Demurrer to Scire Facias

                   This day came the parties by attorneys and thereupon the Defendants Demurrer to the Scire Facias of the plaintiff came on (P-167) for argument. Whereupon all and singular the premises being seen and by the Court fully understood -
    It is considered that said Demurrer be underuled
    And on motion and cause shewn by affidavit Joseph Cutler the defendants are permited to plead which pleas are filed by Defendants Attorney -

The President Directors and)
Company of the Bank of the   )
State of Tennessee   )   Debt.
   VS.   )
William K. Vance and   )
Mordecai Lincoln   )

The Defendants in their proper person appeared in court and confess Judgment according to Specialty - Therefore it is considered that the plaintiffs recover against the Defendants the sum of two hundred and seventy dollars and ninety three cents the Residue of the Specialty declared on with the further sum of Ten Dollars sixty and one half cents for interest due and accrued thereon and their costs by them about their suit in this behalf expended -

On motion of the Attorney General ordered that a Bill of Indictment against Howell Houston and Andrew Stephens be sent to the Grand Jury without a prosecutor (P-168)

Thursday 26th. Octr. 1826

State of Tennessee	)	
William Garrett, Prosr.)		T. A. B. on Delila Garrett
vs.	)	
Jeremiah Jack	)	This day came as well the Attorney

General as the Defendant in his proper person and the Defendant being charged on the Bill of Indictment for plea thereto says that he is not guilty in manner and form as charged in the Bill of Indictment and puts himself on the Country and the Attorney General having done the same came also a jury to wit Robert Leming, Benjamin Brotherton, George Frazier, Cornelius Hughes, Samuel Gass, John Brotherton, Jesse Morgan, Samuel S. Hawkins, Beverly Smith, Moses Harmon, Ellit Rutherford, and Peter Brown who being elected tried and sworn well and truly to try this issue of Traverse upon their oath do say that the Defendant is guilty in manner and form as charged in the Bill of Indictment -- Therefore it is considered that the defendant for such his offence be fined forfeit and pay to the State of Tennessee the sum of fifteen dollars and that he pay the costs of this prosecution - and thereupon came Andrew Stephens Junr. and assumed for and on behalf of the Defendant the payment of the Fine and costs aforesaid and agrees that judgment be entered against him for the same. Therefore it is considered that the State of Tennessee recover against the said Andrew Stephens Junr. the fine and costs aforesaid according to his assumpsit - (P-169)

State of Tennessee	)
Ira Green Prosr.	)
VS.	)
Jacob Hise	)

Assault

Continued as on affidavit James P. Taylor - Jacob Hise acknowledged to owe the State of Tennessee one hundred dollars and James Hise his surety also acknowledged to owe the State of Tennessee fifty dollars yet upon condition that if Jacob Hise shall make his personal appearance at the Court of pleas and quarter sessions to be held for the County of Greene in the Courthouse in Greeneville on Wednesday next after the fourth Monday in January next and stand his trial in this prosecution against him and not depart the court without leave then the above recognizance to be void otherwise in force -

Same, Ira Green prosr.)
   vs.) Assault
Jacob Hise)

                 Continued as on affidavit James
P. Taylor, Jacob Hise acknowledged to owe the State of Tennessee the sum of one hundred dollars and James Hise his surety also acknowledged to owe the State of Tennessee the sum of fifty dollars yet upon condition that if Jacob Hise shall make his personal appearance at theCourt of pleas and quarter Sessions to be held for the county in Greene in the Courthouse in Greeneville on Wednesday next after the fourth Monday in January next. and stand his trial in this prosecution against him and not depart the court without leave then this recognizance to be void otherwise in force –

(P-170) Thursday 26th. Octr. 1826

State of Tennessee)
 E. Rutherford, prosr.) Assault
   vs.)
James Harmon) On motion and with the Assent of
                    the court a Nolli Prosequi is
entered in this prosecution the costs whereof are ordered to be paid by the Defendant. And thereupon James Wyly assumed for and on behalf of the Defendant the payment of the cost aforesaid. Therefore it is considered that the State of Tennessee recover against James W. Wyly the costs aforesaid according to his assumpsit –

Same)
 vs) Assault & Misdemeanor
Same)

      On motion and with the assent of the court a Nolli
prosequi is entered in this prosecution the costs whereof are ordered to be paid by the defendant and thereupon James W. Wyly assumed for and on behalf of the Defendant the payment of the costs aforesaid and agrees that judgment be entered against him for the same – Therefore it is considered that the State of Tennessee recover against the said James W. Wyly the costs aforesaid according to his assumpsit –

State of Tennessee)
   vs.)
Moses Johnson Bail) Sci Fa
of James Long)

      On motion ordered that the forfeiture
in the writ of Scire named be set aside on the payment of the costs by the Defendant and thereupon the said Moses Johnson
(P-171) Johnson assumed the payment of the costs aforesaid Therefore it is considered that the State of Tennessee recover against the said Moses Johnson the costs aforesaid according to his assumpsit

State of Tennessee)
   vs.) Sci Fa Foft. recog.
Moses Johnson Bail)
of James Long)

On motion - ordered that the forfeiture in the writ of
Scire Facias named be set aside on the payment of the costs
by the Defendant and thereupon the Moses Johnson assumed the
the payment of the costs and aforesaid - Therefore it is
considered that the State of Tennessee recovered against the
said Moses Johnson the costs aforesaid according to his
assumpsit -

State of Tennessee)
William Blair Prosr.)
    vs.   )   Assault
Robert McCurry   )

      This day came as well the Attorney
General as the Defendant being charged on the Bill of Indictment /and puts himself on the Country and the Attorney General
having done the same came also a jury to wit John Kennedy,
James Bailey, Jacob Garrett, James Jack, Patrick Coggburn,
Jeremiah Jack, Wyly Craft, David Campbell, James Lowery,
Abraham Brown, Benjamin Smith, Henry Bruner, who being elected
tried and sworn the truth to speak upon the issue of Traverse
upon their oath do say that the Defendant is guilty in manner
and form (P-172) as charged in the Bill of Indictment.

      Therefore it is considered that the Defendant for such
his offence be fined forfeit and pay to the State of Tennessee
one dollar and that he pay the costs of this prosecution -
And Thereupon Joseph McCurry assumed for and on behalf of
the Defendant the payment of the fine and costs aforesaid
and agrees that judgment be entered against him for the same.
Therefore it is considered that the State of Tennessee recover
against the said Joseph McCurry the fine and costs aforesaid
according to his assumpsit - * for plea therefor says that
he is not guilty in manner and form as charged in the Bill

State of Tennessee)   of Indictment
    vs.   )   Sci Fa
John Long Bail   )
of James Long   )   This day came the Attorney General and
                  the Defendant not appearing says noth-
ing in Bar of the Scire Facias of the State whereby the State
recover's against the said defendant therein and ofended.
Therefore it is considered that the State of Tennessee may
have execution against the said John Long for the sum of fifty
dollars the forfeiture in the writ of Scire Facias named, and
that the State of Tennessee also recover against the State of
Tennessee also recover against the said John Long the costs
expended in sueing forth and prosecuting the States writ of
Scire Facias -

State of Tennessee)
    vs.   )   Sci Fa.
John Long Bail   )
of James Long   )   This day came the Attorney General and
                  the Defendant not appearing says noth-
ing in Bar of the Scire Facias of (P.173) the State whereby the State remains against the said John Long the sum of

fifteen dollars the forfeiture in the writ of Scire Facias named and that the State of Tennessee recover against the said John Long the costs expended in sueing forth and prosecuting the States writ of Scire Facias -

State of Tennessee)
Nelly Osburn prosr.)
    vs.   )   T. A. B.
David Campbell   )

    This day came as well the Attorney General as the Defendant in his proper person and the defendant being charged on the bill of Indictment for plea therefor says that he is not guilty in manner and form as therein against him is alledged and puts himself on the Country and the Attorney General having done the same came also a jury to wit, Thomas Harvey, Henry Hoyal, William Inman, Joseph Henry John Hoyal, Absalom Hybarger, Nathan Hoggatt, Thomas Hoge, Thomas Justis, Jacob Gass, Andrew Stephens Junr. William Britton Senr. who being elected tried and sworn the truth to speak upon this issue of Traverse upon their oath do say that the Defendant for such his offence be fined forfeit and pay to the State of Tennessee the sum of ten dollars and that he pay the costs of this prosecution and thereupon came Eliakim Cox and assumed (P-174) for and on behalf of the defendant the payment of the fine and costs aforesaid and agrees that judgment be entered against him for the same - Therefore it is considered that the State of Tennessee recover against the said Eliakim Cox the fine and cost aforesaid according to his assumpsit -

State of Tennessee   )
 David Campbell prosr.)   T. A. B. on Elia Campbell
    vs.   )
Nelly Ausburn   )   This day came as well the Attorney
                       General as the Defendant in her
proper person and the Defendant being charged on the Bill of Indictment for plea thereto says that she is not guilty in manner and form as therein against her is alledged and puts herself on the Country and the Attorney General having done the same came also a jury to wit, Robert Leming, George Frazier, Cornelius Hughes, Samuel S. Hawkins, Beverly Smith, Ezekiel Fox, Robert McCurry, Jacob Newman, John Cook, Emanuel Parman, Thomas Britton, and John Smith who being elected tried and sworn the truth to speak upon this issue of Traverse upon their oath do say that the Defendant is not guilty in manner and form as charged in the Bill of Indictment --

    And on motion and for satisfactory reasons appearing to the Court ordered that the costs of this prosecution be paid by David Campbell the prosecutor - (P-175)

State of Tennessee &)
 William A. Hankins)   Sabbath Breaking
    vs.   )
Absalom Haworth Junr.)   Continued as on affidavit of William

A. Hawkins.

State of Tennessee)
    vs.) Indict as on of Affray
Andrew Stephens Junr.)

    This day came as well the Attorney General as the Defendant being charged on the Bill of Indictment for plea thereto says that he is guilty in manner and form as therein against him is alledged and puts himself on the mercy of the Court that the Defendant for such his offence be fined forfeit and pay to the State of Tennessee the sum of Ten dollars and that he pay the costs of this prosecution - And thereupon came Jeremiah Jacob and assumed for and on behalf of the Defendant the payment of the Fine and costs aforesaid and agrees that judgment be entered against him for the same -

    Therefore it is considered that the State of Tennessee recover against the said Jeremiah Jack the fine and cost aforesaid according to his assumpsit -

Grand and Pettit Jurors discharged 3 days -

(P-176)   Thursday 26th. Octr. 1826

State of Tennessee)
    vs.) Affray
Howel Houston)

    This day came as well the Attorney General as the Defendant in his proper person and the Defendant being charged on the bill of Indictment for plea thereto says that he is guilty in manner and form as therein against him is alledged and puts himself on the mercy of the Court. Therefore it is considered that the Defendant for such his offence be find forfeit and pay to the State of Tennessee the sum of ten dollars and that he pay the costs of this prosecution - and thereupon Andrew Susong Senr. assumed for and on behalf of the Defendant the payment of the Fine and costs aforesaid and agrees that judgment be entered against him for the same. Therefore it is considered that the State of Tennessee recover against the said Andrew Susong Senr. the fine and costs aforesaid according to his assumpsit -

State of Tennessee)
    vs.) Bastardy
Abraham Sellers)

    The Defendant who stands bound by recognizance for his appearance here at the present court to answer the State of Tennessee of a charge alledged against him for begetting a Bastard child of the body of Rachel Stiegel of this County single woman appeared according and entered into Bond in the sum of six hundred dollars with Finch, Peter Sellers and Jotham Brown (P-177) Junr. Securities conditioned that the said Defendant shall perform such order as the Court shall from time to time make concerning the maintainance of said child and indemnify the County of Greene free from all charges in consequence of the birth and maintainance of the same according to Law.

Whereupon it is ordered that the Defendant pay the costs in this behalf expended -

And Court adjourned untill tomorrow morning 9 o'clock

Joseph Brown, J.P.
M. Lincoln, J.P.
Leonard Starnes

Friday 27th. October 1826

Court met present.

The Minutes of Yesterday proceedings were read and signed-

Rachael Stiegel)
vs.) Motion for Allowance
Abraham Sellers &)
Aaron Finch) The plaintiff by her Attorney James P.
Taylor moved Court here for an allow-
ance for the maintainance of a Bastard child (P-178) against the defendant and securties whereupon it is considered that the plaintiff recover against the said Abraham Sells, Aaron Finch, Peter Sellers and Jotham Brown Junr. his securities the sum of forty dollars for her one year allowance for the maintainance of a Bastard child begoten of the body of Rachel Stiegel by the said Abraham Sellers and the costs of this motion -

State of Tennessee)
vs.) Sci Fa. foft. recog.
James Long)

On motion - ordered that the forfeiture in this writ of Scire Facias named be set aside the costs of which are assumed be set aside by the Defendant. And There-upon it is considered that the State of Tennessee recover against the said Jesse Morgan, ReubinLong and William Long the costs aforesaid according to his assumpsit

Execution staid 8 months

Same)
vs.) Sci Fa. forfeited recognizance
Same)

On motion ordered that the forfeiture in this writ of Scire Facias named be set aside the costs of which are assumed by the Defendant in his proper peron - And thereupon Reubin Long, Jesse Morgan and William Long assumed for and on behalf of the Defendant the payment of the costs, afore-said and agree that judgment be entered (P-179) against them for the same. Therefore it is considered that the State of Tennessee recover against the said Reubin Long, Jesse Morgan and William Long the costs aforesaid according to their assumpsit--

Execution staid 8 months

State of Tennessee)
     vs.   )   Sci Fa. Foft. Recog.
John Long Bail of)
  James Long   )   On motion and with the assent of the
                      court - ordered that the judgment
Ni Si entered against the defendant at the present term
this court be set aside on the payment of the costs by said
Defendant and thereupon Reubin Long, Jesse Morgan, and William Long assumed for and on behalf of the Defendant the payment of the costs aforesaid and agree that judgment be entered against them for the same - Therefore it is considered
that the State of Tennessee recover against the said Reubin
Long, Jesse Morgan, and William Long the costs aforesaid according to their assumpsit -
                   Execution stand 8 months

Same   )
 vs.   )   Sci Fa. Forfeited Recognizance
Same   )

       On motion and with the assent of the court the Defend-
ant at the present Term of this court be set aside on the payment of the costs by said Defendant - and thereupon Reubin Long
Jesse Morgan and William Long assumed for and behalf of the
Defendant the payment of the costs aforesaid and agree that
judgment be entered against them for the same - Therefore it
is considered that the State (P-180) of Tennessee recover
against the said Reubin Long, Jesse Morgan and William Long
the costs aforesaid according to their assumpsit -
                   Execution staid 8 months

State of Tennessee)
    vs.   )   Indict. for Blasphemy
James Long   )

       On motion and with the assent of the
Court a Nolli Proseque is entered in this prosecution the costs
of which is assumed by the defendant and thereupon came Reubin
Long, Jesse Morgan, and William Long and assumed for and on
behalf of the Defendant the payment of the costs aforesaid
and agree the judgment be entered against them for the same -
Therefore it is considered that the State of Tennessee recover
against the said Reubin Long, Jesse Morgan and William Long
the costs aforesaid according to his assumpsit -
                   Execution staid 8 months

Eliza Hays an Infant &c.)
by Joseph Hays her father)   Case for wards
and next Friend   )
    vs.   )   Joseph Hays by James W. Wyly his
Frederick Row   )   Attorney dismisses this suit and
                    assumes the costs - Therefore it
is considered that the said Joseph Hays pay the costs in this
behalf expended -

Eliza Hays and Infant who)
sues by Joseph Hays her   )   Case for Wards
father and next Friend   )

Eliza Hays and Infant who)
sues by Joseph Hays her)
father and next friend) Case for Wards
  vs.)
Levi Baxter and wife) Joseph Hays by James W. Wyly
        (P-181) his attorney dismisses
his suit and assumes the cost - Therefore it is considered
that the said Joseph Hays pay the costs in this behalf expended-

Eliza Hays and Infant &c.)
who sues by Joseph Hays)
her father and next Friend) Case for Wards
  vs.)
Sally Row) Joseph Hays by his attorney,
      James W. Wyly dismisses his
suit and assumes the cost. Therefore it is considered that
the said Joseph Hays pay the costs in this behalf expended -

Thomas Harvey)
  vs.) Certio
John Thomason)
    On motion ordered that the order of References
made in this cause at the last Term of this Court be set aside

John Gillespie)
  vs.) Assumpsit Demurrer to Declaration
Allen Gillespie)
    The Defendant by Attorney withdraws the
Demurrer heretofore failed to the plaintiffs Declaration and
on motion of plaintiff by Attorney he is permited to amend -

Jacob Smelsor)
  vs.) Debt
William M. P. Mitchell &)
Moses G. Wilson) On motion of Defendants by
     (P-182) Attorney they are per-
mitted to file at this time a Demurrer to the Declaration
of the plaintiff.
    Whereupon argument of Counsel being heard and all and
singular the premises being seen and by the Court fully understood. It is considered that said Demurrer be sustained and
that the Defendants recover against the plaintiff their costs
by them about their defence in this behalf expended -

State of Tennessee)
Henry Tanant, Prosr.) Recognized for Perjury
  vs.)
Alexander Dugger) The papers in this prosecution being
     returned by Mordecai Lincoln, esquire
the Justice of the Peace by whom the recognizance were taken.
   It is ordered that the Defendant be discharged from his
Recognizance

William Senter & Thomas Hale)
Exers. of Nehemiah Pettit decd.)   Debt
            vs.   )
Valentine Ketring, Jacob Kinsor)   Christian Harman appearances
Adam Ketring and Henry Fry   )   Ball of Valentine Ketring
                                     in this suit produced and
surrendered in open court the body of the said Valentine Ketring
in discharge of himself as Bail –

(P-183) Friday 27th. Octr. 1826
Valentine Sevier Surviving   )
partner of Deaderick & Sevier   )
Assignees of Michael Myers   )   Covenant – Indict.
for the use of Jacob A. Deadrick)   Attachment.
            vs.   )
Joseph Rutherford and James Rutherford) This day came the plain-
the Defendants although solemnly called came not but made default. Therefore it is considered that the plaintiff recover
recover against the Defendant his damages by occasion in the
Declaration mentioned but because it is unknown to the Court
what those Damages are – It is ordered that a jury came here
at the next Term of this court to inquire of Damages between
the parties in this suit --

John Kennedy   )
    vs.   )   Scire Facias
Henry Dyche,   )
Michael Dyche   )   Christian Dyche, John Dyche, John Dyche
                 William H. Moore, & Catharine his wife
Nathaniel D. Moore & Peggy his wife Elizabeth Dyche and Christiana Dyche Heirs of Henry Dyche Dec'd.
    This day came the plaintiff by Seth Luckey his attorney
and the Scire Facias awarded in this cause being returned
executed and the Defendants not appearing nor is anything
said in Bar of the said writ of Scire Facias – It is therefore considered by the court that the plaintiff may have execution of his judgment in the said writ of Scire Facias mentioned
(P-184) against the real estate of the said Henry Dyche Decd
in the bonds of the said heirs and his cost expended in sueing
forth and prosecuting his said writ of Scire Facias.

Hugh Malony   )
    vs.   ) Ca. Sa. Issued by Justice
Christian Dyche &   )
William S. Perry   ) From the judgment rendered in this cause
                        at the present term of this court the
Defendants by Attorney prays an appeal to the next court of
Law to be held for the County of Greene in the Courthouse in
Greenville on the first Monday in March next – and having
given bond and security to prosecute –their appeal is granted
and the proceedings ordered to be certified –

    The President & Directors   )
& Company of the Bank of the   )
State of Tennessee   )
    Vs.   )   Debt.
William K. Vance & Valentine Sevier)

Alexander Sevier the principal Debtor and on his motion by Attorney is admitted a joint defendant in this action - the Court being satisfied that the said defendants William K. Vance and Valentine Sevier have sufficient colleteral Security as appeared from Deed of Trust executed to Hugh Carter -

Henry Feazle   )
   vs.   )   Certio
Moses G. Wilson)

          This day came the Defendant by Attorney and the plaintiff although solemnly (P-185) came not let made default. Therefore it is considered that the plaintiff now pleas. and that the Defendant go hence and Recover against the plaintiff his costs by him about his defence in this behalf expended

Mordecae Lincoln)
   vs.   ) Order Sale
Joseph Rutherford)

          Richard M. Woods High Sheriff of Green County Returns into Court an Execution issued by Alexander Brown Keeper of Justice Records for Said County Against the Estate of the Defendant for the sum of four dollars twenty and one half cents debt and the further sum of one dollar twenty five cents cost recovered by the plaintiff the Defendant before Richard West, Esquire there an acting justice of the peace for said on the 9th. day of March 1825 on which. Execution said constable has made Return, there is no personal property found by me in my county therefore I have levied on all the Right title and claims that Joseph Rutherford has as heir of Eliott Rutherford Deceased to the following tracts of land undivided lying on Gap Creek on the north side of Lick Creek one tract of one hundred and fifty three acres one of thirty seven acres and one of ten acres more or less joining each other including the place where Ruth Rutherford now lives and joining the land of Eliott Rutherford Jr. also one hundred acres joining the said Rutherford and Jesse Self 17th. October 1826 R. M. Woods Shff." therefore on motion of the plaintiff by John A. Ackin his Attorney it is considered by the court that the undivided interest of the said Joseph Rutherford of in and (P-186) To the aforesaid Tracts of Land so levied on be condemned to the satisfaction of the Recovery aforesaid and that the Same or so much thereof as will satisfy said Recovery and the cost of this motion be sold as the law directs

State of Tennessee)
   vs.   ) Sci Fa. Forftd. Recog.
Levi Babb Bail of)
Ira Greene   )

          This day came the Attorney General and the Defendant not appearing says nothing in Bar of the Scire Facias of the State whereby the State Remains against the said Defendant therein undefeated Thereof it is considered that the State of Tennessee may have Execution against the said Levi Babb for the sum of one hundred dollars Forfeiture in the writ of Scire Facias named and that the State of Tennessee also recover against the said Defendant the costs Expended in sueing forth prosecuting the State writ of Scire Facias.

Same)
vs.) Sci Fa Foftd. Recognizance
Same)

     This day came the Attorney General General and the Defendant not appearing says nothing in Bar of the Scire Facias of the State whereby the State Remains against the said Defendant therein undefinded Therefore it is considered that the State of Tennessee may have Execution against the said Levi Babb for the sum of one hundred dollars the forfeiture in the writ of Scire Facias named and that the State of Tennessee also recover against the the said Defendant the costs expended in sueing (P-187) forth and presenting the State writ of Scire Facias -

Valentine Sevier Surviving)
Partner of Deaderick & Sevier)   Order Sale
for William H. Deaderick)
   vs.)   Richard M. Woods, High
James Rutherford)   Sheriff of Greene County
                               returned here into court
on execution issued by Mordecai Lincoln, esquire an acting justice of the peace for said County against the estate of the Defendant for the sum of Seventeen dollars and fifty eight cents debt and fifty cents costs, recovered by the plaintiff against the defendant before said justice on the 30th. day of September 1826 on which execution said constable has made return "Search made and no personal property found in my County. Therefore I have levied on all the right title and claim that James Rutherford has (as heir of Elliott Rutherford decd of in and to the following tracts of land lying on Gap Creek on the north side of Lick Creek one tract of one hundred and fifty three acres one tract of one hundred acres one of thirty seven acres and one of ten acres each more or less three of the tracts joining each other including the place where Ruth Rutherford now lives and the hundred acres tract bounded by the tract of Elliott Rutherford and Jesse Self 20th. October 1826 R. M. Woods Shff. Therefore on motion of the plaintiff by John A. Aiken his attorney It is considered by the court that all right title and claim which James Rutherford has of in and to the aforesaid Tracts of land so levied on be condemned to the Satisfaction of the Recovery aforesaid (P-138) and that the same or so much thereof as will satisfy said Recovery and the costs of this motion be sold as the law directs -

Robert Rhea)
   vs.) Order Sale -
Robert Rutherford)

     Richard M. Woods, High Sheriff of Greene

County returned here into court an execution issued by
Alexander Brown Keeper of Justices Records of said County
against the estate of the Defendant for the sum of Two
dollars forty five and a half cents Debt and one dollar
and twenty five cents cost recovered by the plaintiff
against the Defendant before Richard West, esquire then
an acting justice of the peace for said County on the 15th.
day of April 1826 - On which execution said constable has
made return "Search made and no personal property found in
my County therefore I have levied on all the right, title
and interest that Robert Rutherford has as heir of Elliott
Rutherford decd. to the following tracts of land lying on
Gap Creek undivided - One tract of one hundred and fifty
three acres one tract of thirty seven acres and one of ten
acres all joining each other and joining the lands of
Elliott Rutherford Junr. including the place where Ruth
Rutherford now lives also one other tract of one hundred
acres on Gap Creek joining the lands of Elliott Rutherford
and Jesse Self 17th. October 1826. R. M. Woods Shff.
"Therefore on motion of the plaintiff by John A. Aiken his
Attorney It is considered that the aforesaid undivided
Interest of the said Robert Rutherford of in and the tracts
of land levied on as aforesaid be condemned to the satisfaction of the recovery aforesaid and that the same or
(P-189) so much thereof as will satisfy said recovery and
the costs of this motion be sold as the law directs -
     And Court adjourned untill court in course untill
which time all matters and things in the same depending
and undetermined are continued
                              M. Lincoln
                              Justice of the peace
                              Joseph Brown, J.P.

(P-190)   State of Tennessee:
                    At a Court of Pleas and Quarter
Sessions continued and held for the County of Greene in
the Courthouse in Greeneville on the fourth Monday being
the 23rd. day of January one thousand eight hundred and
Twenty Seven.
                    Was Present.

William M. P. Mitchell)
     vs.   ) Certio
John Graham   )
                    The petition of the Defendant
was presented by James W. Wyly his attorney praying writs of
Certiorari and Supersedeas upon consideration whereof It
is ordered that writs issue pursuant to the prayer of said
petition returnable here at our next court on Bond and
Security being given according to Law -

Barnabas Hawk   )
     vs.   ) Order Sale
Letitia Jackson)
                    Humphries well a constable of Greene County
returned here into Court an execution issued by George Wells

esquire, an acting Justice of the Peace for said County against the estate of the Defendant before said justice on the 30th. day of December last past for the sum of Twelve Dollars and Thirty Cents Debt and fifty cents on which execution said constable has made return no goods or chattels of the said Letitia Jackson the Defendant to be found in my County therefore and this execution an all the right title interest claim and demand that she has of in and to two entries (P-191) of land - one containing twenty four and the other fifty acres being the same more or less lying in Greene County on the Waters of Cove Creek joining John Love, William Lawson and other the 13th. day of January 1827

Humphries Wells

Therefore on motion of the plaintiff it is considered that the aforesaid two entries of land so levied on be condemned to the satisfaction of the recovery aforesaid and that the same or so much thereof as will satisfy said recovery and the costs of this motion be sold as the law directs-

Jacob Statts)
    vs.) Order Sale
Letitia Jackson)

Humphries Wells a constable of Greene County returned here into open court and execution issued by George Wells, esquire an acting justice of the peace for said County against the Estate of the Defendant for the sum of eight Dollars twelve and one half cents recovered by the plaintiff against the Defendant before said justice on the (9th. day of January 1827 on which execution said constable has made return "no goods or chattels of the said Letitia Jackson the Defendant to be found in my County therefore levied the execution on all the right title claim and demand that she has of in and to two entries of land one containing twenty four acres and the other fifty acres be the same more or less lying Greene County on the waters of Cove Creek joining John Love, William Lawson and others-

Therefore on motion of the plaintiff it is considered that the aforesaid two entries of land so laid on be condemned to the satisfaction of the Recovery aforesaid and that the same or so much thereof as well satisfy said (P-192) recovery and the costs of this motion be sold as the law directs -

And Court adjourned until tomorrow 10 o'clock

M. Lincoln, J.P.
Thos. Hale, J.P.
A. Gillespie, J.P.

Tuesday 23rd. Jany 1827

Court Sat   Present:

The Minutes of yesterdays proceedings were read and signed -

James Gillespie)
    vs.) Case in Assumpsit
Allen Gillespie)

    By consent the matters in dispute between the parties in this suit are refered to the final determination of Henry Earnest, Stephen Brooks and Samuel Snapp who award thereupon is to be made the judgment of the Court which is ordered accordingly -

George Bell)
    vs.) Certio
Henry A. Farnsworth)

                Continued by consent

(P-193)   Tuesday 23rd. Jany. 1827

Daniel M. Guin)
    vs.) Appeal
Ephraim Wilson Exor.)

                Continued as on special affidavit
of Defendant.

Isaac Humbard)
    vs.) Certio
James Hise)

    On motion of Defendant by Attorney Alias Writs of Certiorari and Supersedeas are awarded him returnable here at next Court.

    Richard M. Woods esquire high sheriff in and for the County of Greene returns here into open Court the States writ of Venire Facias to him directed endorsed "Returnable Tuesday after the fourth Monday in January 1827. Issd. 31st. October 1826. Recd.31st. October executed on all but Samuel Henderson, Johnson Frazier, Frederick Myers, Adam Painter R. M. Woods Shff" out of whom are selected as the Statutes in that case provides the following persons a Grand Inquest and Jury to wit
    Jacob Broyles appointed foreman by the Court

Meshach Hail   James Smith
Benjamin D. Browning   John Coggburn
Samuel Carter   Samuel Grubbs
Solomon Wampler   Philip Fry
David Standfield   John Lester &
Emanuel Dyche   Abraham B. Bowen

good and lawful men of the County of Greene received their charge and retired from the Bar. (P-194) Leeland Davis a constable was qualified to attend on the Grand Jury
    2 days certi issd. I, Davis, Duplicate issd. to Jones & Greenway who have mislaid the former cost 27th Feb. 1829.
                (2 days each)

    Turner Smith a Constable to attend on the Court.
                3 days certif. issd.
                Wm. K. Vance.

James Bell, Peter Couch, and Andrew Smilie the Residue of the Venire to the present Court are to attend the same respectively as pettit jurors untill discharged.

On motion and for satisfactory reasons appearing to the court. Ordered that Andrew Stephens Senr. Jesse Self, John Gladin, George Loones, and William Evans be severally released from further attendance at the present court as jurors.

William McDannel)
    vs.   ) Debt
Jacob Newman   )

This day came the parties by attornies and thereupon a jury to wit James Bell, Peter Couch, George Bell, Nathan Hawkins, Peter Whittenburg, William Blair, Ephraim Wilson, Jacob Eddleman, Henry Fry, Wyly Craft, David E. W. Babb, and Philip Babb Junr. who being elected tried and sworn well and truly to try this cause upon their oath do say that the Defendant has paid the Debt in the Declaration mentioned except the sum of one hundred seven dollars and sixty six cents and they do assess the plaintiffs Damages by reason of the Detention of said Debt to seven dollars and sixty six cents. Therefore it is considered that the plaintiff recover against the defendant the aforesaid sum of one hundred seven dollars sixty six cents (P-195) the residue of the Debt in the Declaration mentioned with the Damages by the jury aforesaid assessed and his costs by him about his suit in this behalf expended -

State and William A. Hankins)
    vs.   ) Sabbath Breaking
Absalom Haworth   )

The plaintiff William A. Hankins by his written order filed dismisses his suit and assumes the payment of one third of the costs and the Defendant assumes the payment of the remaining two thirds of the cost. Therefore it is considered that the parties recover against each other according to their assumpsits -

John Baker   )
   vs.   ) Certio
Howell Houston and)
William Houston   ) On motion and cause shewn by affidavit of Defendants this cause is
continued untill next Court.

John Love   )
  vs.   ) Certio
George Welty)

On motion of Plaintiff by Attorney a Rule is allowed him to shew cause why the Defendants petition should be dismissed -

John Balch   )
   vs.   ) Certio
James McPherran)

On motion and cause shewn by affidavit
plaintiff this cause is continued untill the next Term of
this Court.

(P-196)
Jacob T. Wyrick)
   vs.   ) Certio
Andrew Park   )

By consent the matters in dispute between
the parties in this suit are refered to the final determination of Moses G. Wilson on and Thos. Murphey with liberty of
choosing and----should theydisagree whose award thereupon
is to be made the judgment of the court which is ordered
accordingly -

Samuel Jackson   )
assignee Jno. A. Aiken) Covenant
   vs.   )
Howell Houston   ) John Guin appearance Bail of the
                         Defendant in discharge of himself
as Bail - Whereupon John Gladin appeared in court and assumed
for and on behalf of the said Defendant that if he shall be
cast in this suit that he will pay the costs and condemna-
tion or that he the said John Gladin will do it for him -

Thomas Harvey)
   vs.   ) Certio
John Thomason)

This day came the parties by attornies
and thereupon a jury to wit James Bell, Peter Couch, George
Bell, Peter Whittenburg, William Blair, Ephraim Wilson,
Jacob Addleman, Henry Fry, Wyly Craft, David E. W. Babb,
Philip Babb Junr. and Martin Cline who being (P-197)
Tuesday 23rd. Jany 1827 elected tried and sworn well and
truly to try this cause - The Defendant by Attorney moved
the court to quash the proceedings before the justice and
on argument the court ordered the proceedings before the
justice of the peace to be quash and the jury for rendering
their verdict to be discharged - and thereupon it was considered that the plaintiff take nothing by his suit and that
the defendant recover against the plaintiff his costs by him
about his suit in this behalf expended -
From which Judgment the plaintiff by Attorney prays an
appeal in the nature of a writ of error to the next circuit
court of law to be held for the County of Greene in the Courthouse in Greeneville on the first Monday in March next and
having given Bond and Security to prosecute his appeal is
granted and the proceedings ordered to be certified -
During the progress of this suit plaintiff tenders his
bill of exceptions & which is signed and sealed and ordered
to be part of record
And Court adjourned until tomorrow morning 9 o'clock

L. Ball
Nenny Dyche
Leonard Starnes

(P-198)   Wednesday 24th. January 1827

Court met present

The Minutes of yesterdays proceedings were read and signed.

State of Tennessee   )
Sparling Bowman, prosr.)   T. A. B.
    vs.   )
Philip Cummings   )   This day came as well the Attorney
                                    General as the Defendant being
charged on the Bill of Indictment for plea thereto says that
he is guilty in manner and form as therein against him is
alledged and puts himself on the mercy of the Court. Therefore it is considered that the Defendant for such offence
be fined forfeit and pay to the State of Tennessee the sum
of one dollar and that he pay the costs of this prosecution.
And thereupon came William Nelson and assumed for and on
behalf of the Defendant the payment of the fine and costs
aforesaid and agrees that judgment be entered against him
for the same - Therefore it is considered that the State
of Tennessee recover against the said William Nelson the
fine costs aforesaid according to his assumpsit --

(P-199)   Wednesday 24th. January 1827
Valentine Sevier sureving partner)
of Deaderick & Sevier for   ) Covenant
the use of Alexander Anderson   )
    vs.   ) Demurrer to Declaration
John Guin and Daniel Guin   )
                                    This day came the
parties by Attornies and thereupon the Defendants Demurrer
to the Plaintiffs Declaration came on for argument. Whereupon all and singular the premises being seen and by the
Court fully understood. It is considered that said Demurrer
(be overuled) and that the plaintiff recover against the
Defendant his Damages by occasion in the Declaration mentioned Damages are -   It is ordered that a jury came here at
the next term of this court to enquire of damages between
the parties

The President Directors & Co.   )
of the Bank of the State of Tenn.)   The death of David Mc-
    vs.   )   Cord, one of the Def-
David McCord, George T. Gillespie)   endants suggested -
and Alfred Hunter   and thereupon George
                                      T. Gillespie appeard
in Court and confesses judgment for the sum of one hundred
thirty six dollars and eighty three cents - Therefore it
is considered that the plaintiff recover against the said

George T. Gillespie, the aforesaid sum of one hundred thirty
six dollars and eighty three cents and their costs by them
about their suit in this behalf expended --

(P-200) Wednesday 24th. 1827
State of Tennessee   )
Sparling Bowman, prosr.)   T. A. B.
        vs.   )
Peter Laney   ) This day came as well the Attorney
                                  General as the Defendant in his
proper person and the Defendant being charged on the Bill of
Indictment for plea thereto says that he is guilty in manner
and form as therein against him is alledged and puts himself
on the mercy of the Court. Therefore it is considered that
the Defendant for such his offence be fined forfeit and pay
to the State of Tennessee the sum of this prosecution - and
thereupon came Ephraim Laney and assumed for and on behalf of
the Defendant the payment of the fine and costs aforesaid and
agrees that judgment be entered against him for the same.
        Therefore it is considered that the State of Tennessee
recover against the said Ephraim Laney the fine and costs
aforesaid according to his assumpsit -

State of Tennessee   )
Charles Evans, prosr.)   T. A. B.
    vs.   )
Benedict Hoyal   )   This day came as well the Attorney
                                  General as the Defendant in his
proper person and the Defendant being charged on the Bill of
Indictment for plea thereto says that he is guilty in manner
and form as charged in the bill of Indictment and puts himself on the mercy of the court - Therefore it is considered
that the defendant for such his offence be fined forfeit
(P-201) and pay the State of Tennessee the sum of twenty five
cents and that he pay the costs of this prosecution - and
thereupon came Evin Henry and assumed for and on behalf of
the Defendant the payment of the fine and costs aforesaid
and agrees that judgment It is considered that the State of
Tennessee recover against the said Evin Henry the fine and
costs aforesaid according to his assumpsit --

Henry Earnest & Co.)
    vs.   )   Case
John Davis   )
                        This day came the parties by attornies
and thereupon a jury to wit James Bell, Peter Couch, Thomas
Lasson, Ephraim Laney, Thomas Crutchfield, Thomas David,
Benjamin Bowman, Samuel K. Gauntt, William Nelson, Thomas
Dodd, Henry Henegar and Jeremiah Casteel who being elected
tried and sworn the truth to speak upon the issue joined
upon their oath do say that the Defendant did assume in manner
and form as the plaintiff against him in his declaration both
complained and they do assess the plaintiff Damages by
accasion thereof to two hundred dollars and on motion of Defendant by Attorney a rule is allowed him to shew cause why
a new trial should be granted.

(P-202)   Wednesday 24th. Jany. 1827.

John Robinson for   )
Samuel Caldwell use   )   Covt.
     vs.   )
James Tadlock and   )   This day came the parties by attor-
Thomas Caldwell   )   nies and thereupon a jury to wit
                                 James Bell, Peter Couch, Thomas
Lesson, Ephraim Laney, Thomas Cruthfield, Thomas Davis,
Benjamin Bowman, Samuel K. Gauntt, William Nelson, Thomas
Dodd, Henry Honegar and Jeremiah Casteel who being elected
tried and sworn well and truly to enquire of Damages between the parties upon their oath do say that the plaintiff
hath sustained damages by occasion in the Declaration mentioned to the sum of one hundred and eight dollars and fifty
cents.   Therefore it is considered that the plaintiff recover
against the Defendants the aforesaid sum of one hundred and
eight dollars and fifty cents the Damages by the jury assessed
and their costs by them about their suit in this behalf expended -

George Weems and Hannah Weems)
Administrator of James Weems   )   Debt
dec'd for the use of Allen Ross)
     vs.   )
Jesse Kirby & Christopher Kerby)   This day came the parties
                                     by attornies and thereupon
                                     a jury to wit James Bell,
Peter Couch, Thomas Lawson, Thomas Lawson, Ephraim Laney,
Thomas Crutchfield, Thomas Davis, Benjamin Bowman, Samuel K.
Gauntt, William Nelson, Thomas Dodd, Henry Honegar, and
Jeremiah Casteel, who being elected tried and sworn well and
truly to try this cause upon their oath do (P-205) say that
the Defendants have not paid the Debt in the Declaration
mentioned as in pleading they have alledged and they do
assess the plaintiffs damages by reason of the Detention of
said Debt to nineteen dollars and fifty cents - Therefore
it is considered that the plaintiff recover against the
Defendants the sum of eighty seven dollars and seventy six
cents the debt in the declaration mentioned with the damages
by the jury aforesaid assessed and his costs by him about
his suit in this behalf expended -

Valentine Sevier surviving partner)
of Deaderick & Sevier for the   )   Writ of Enquiry Covt.
use of Joseph Deaderick   )   Indct. Attachment
     vs.   )
Joseph Rutherford and   )   This day came the plain-
James Rutherford   )   tiff by Attorney and
                                          thereupon a jury to wit
James Bell, Peter Couch, Thomas Lawson, Ephraim Laney, Thomas
Crutchfield, Thomas Davis, Benjamin Bowman, Samuel K. Gauntt
William Nelson, Thomas Dodd, Henry Henegar and Jeremiah Casteel who being elected tried and sworn well and truly to
enquire of Damages between the parties upon their oath do
say that the plaintiffs has sustained damages by occasion
in the Declaration mentioned to the amount of one hundred

Dollars and eighty seven cents -
Therefore it is considered that the plaintiff recover against the Defendants the aforesaid sum of one hundred dollars and eighty seven cents and his costs by him about his suit in this behalf expended. (P-204)

Wednesday 24th. Jany. 1827

Alexander Anderson)
assignee &c.   ) Debt
   vs.   )
George Brown   ) On motion and cause shewn by affidavit
                  of Defendant   this cause is continued
until next Court -

State of Tennessee   )
Sparling Bowman, Prosr.) T. A. B.
   vs.   )
Enoch Light   ) This day came as well the Attorney
                 General as the Defendant in his
proper person and the Defendant being charged on the bill of Indictment for plea thereto says that he is guilty in manner and form as therein against him is alledged and puts himself on the mercy of the court Therefore it is considered that the Defendant for such his offence be fined forfeit and pay to the State of Tennessee the sum of two dollars and fifty cents and that he pay the costs of this prosecution and thereupon came John Light and assumed for and on behalf of the Defendant the payment of the fine and costs aforesaid and agrees that the judgment be entered against him for the same Therefore it is considered that the State of Tennessee recover against the said John Light the fine and costs aforesaid according to his assumpsit - (P-205)

Henry Earnest & Co.)
   vs.   ) Case Verdict for Plaintiff and Rule
John Davis   )   for new Trial.
                 This day came the parties by attornies and thereupon the rule entered to shew cause why a new trial should be granted came on for argument whereupon all and singular the premises being seen and by the court fully understood. It is considered that said rule be discharged and that the plaintiff recover against the Defendant the sum of Two Dollars the Damages assessed by the jury and their cost by them and their suit in this behalf expended -

State of Tennessee)
Ira Green, Prosr.   ) Assault
   vs.   )
Jacob Hise   ) This day came the Defendant in his
                 proper person and the Defendant being charged on the Bill of Indictment for plea thereto says that he is not guilty in manner and form as charged in the Bill of Indictment and puts himself on the Country and the Attorney General having done the same came also a jury to wit Andrew Smiley, Jack Stephens, Samuel Stephens, David Logan

George Rightsell, John Light, Martin Cline, William H. Mc Coy, John Baker, Emanuel Parman, Wyly Craft and Barnabas Hawk who being elected tried and sworn the truth to speak upon their issue Traverse upon their oath do say that the defendant is not guilty in manner and form as charged in the Bill of Indictment - and on motion and for reason appearing to the court ordered that the costs of this prosecution be paid by the prosecution -

(P-206)   Wednesday 24th. Jany. 1827

Henry Earnest & Co.) vs.) John Davis)	Debt. Demurrer to Declaration

This day came the parties by attornies and thereupon the Defendants Demurrer to the plaintiffs Declaration came on for argument whereupon all and singular the premises being seen and by the court fully understood. It is considered that said Demurrer be overruled and that the plaintiffs recover against the Defendant the sum of one hundred and fifty dollars and eighty two cents the debt in the Declaration mentioned with interest thereon at the rate of six pr. centerun pr. annum from the 19th. day of February 1825 and their costs by them about their suit in this behalf expended -

John Baker) vs.) Peter Brown and) Jack Dyche)	T. A. B. The plaintiff by Attorney entered a non suit as to Jacob Dyches one of the Defend-

ants -
And thereupon came the parties by Attornies and thereupon a jury to wit Jacob Carter, Samuel Babb, George Smith, Daniel Carter Junr. Absalom Stone-Cypher, John Malony, Christian Cook, Thomas Justis, Sparling Bowman, David Good, Lemuel Jones, and Dutton Lane, who being elected tried and sworn well and truly to try this cause-
The Plaintiff by Attorney suffers a Non Suit - And on motion of Plaintiff by Attorney a Rule is allowed him to shew   (P-207) cause why the non suit should be set aside -

State of Tennessee) Bryant Deaton Prosr.) vs.) Peter Brown)	T. A. B. Continued as on special affidavit of the prosecutor - Peter Brown acknowledged to owe the State of

Tennessee two hundred and fifty dollars and Tilman A. Howard his surety also acknowledge to owe the State of Tennessee the sum of one hundred dollars - Yet upon condition that if Peter Brown shall make his personal appearance at the Court of pleas and quarter sessions to be held for the County of Greene in the Courthouse in Greenville on Wednesday next

after the fourth Monday inApril next and stand his trial
this prosecution against him and not depart the court without leave then the above recognizance to be void otherwise
in force - Bryant Deaton the prosecutor also acknowledged
to owe the State of Tennessee the sum of one hundred dollars
yet upon conditions that he shall make his personal appearance at the Court of Pleas and quarter sessions to be held
for the County of Greene in the Courthouse in Greeneville
on Wednesday next after the fourth Monday in April next
and prosecute and give evidence on behalf of the State of
Tennessee in this prosecution against Peter Brown and not
depart the Court without leave then the above recognizance
to be void otherwise in force. (P-203) Wednesday 24, Jany.
1827.

State of Tennessee   )
Bryant Deaton, Prosr.)   T. A. B.
    vs.   )
James Johnson   )   Continued as on special affidavit
                          of prosecution - James Johnson
acknowledged to owe the State of Tennessee Two hundred and
fifty Dollars and Tilman A. Howard his Security also acknowledged to owe the State of Tennessee one hundred dollars -
Yet upon condition that if James Johnson shall make his
personal appearance at the Court of Pleas and Quarter Session to be held for the County of Greene in the Courthouse in
Greeneville on Wednesday next after the fourth Monday in
April next and stand his trial in this prosecution against
him and not depart the court without leave then the above
recognizance to be void otherwise in force - Bryant Deaton
the prosecutor also acknowledge to owe the State of Tennessee
the sum of one hundred dollars yet upon conditions that if
he shall make his personal appearance at the Court of pleas
and quarter Sessions to be held for the County of Greene in
the Courthouse in Greeneville on Wednesday next after the
fourth Monday in April next and prosecute and give evidence
on behalf of the State of Tennessee in this prosecution and
not depart the court without leave then this recognizance to
be void otherwise in force -   (P-209)

     Wednesday 24th. Jany. 1827.
State of Tennessee)
  Ira Greene, Prosr.)   Assault
    vs.   )
Jacob Hise   )   Continued on affidavit of Defendant
                        Jacob Hise acknowledged to owe to
the State of Tennessee one hundred dollars and James Hise
his surety also acknowledged to owe to the State of Tennessee
fifty dollars - Yet upon condition that if he the said Jacob
Hise shall make his personal appearance at the Court of pleas
and quarter sessions to be held for the County of Greene in
the Courthouse in Greeneville on Wednesday next after the
fourth Monday in April next and stand his trial in this prosecution against him and not depart the Court without leave
then the above recognizance to be void otherwise in force -

State of Tennessee)
John Commins, Prosr.)
    vs.   )   Assault offered to Nancy Cummings
John Rymal   )

        The Defendant who stands bound by
recognizance in the sum of one hundred dollars for his
appearance here to answer a charge of the State against
was solemnly called for that purpose but came not and made
default - Therefore it is considered that the State of
Tennessee recover against the said John Rymal the sum of
one hundred dollars the amount of his recognizance in this
behalf acknowledged unless sufficient cause for such failure
be shewn - George House, who stands bound by recognizance
in the sum of fifty dollars for the appearance of John Rymal
to answer a charge of the State   (P-210)   against him was
solemnly called to bring into the Court the body of the said
John Rymal and surrender the same in discharge of himself as
Bail but failed so to do whereupon it is considered that the
State of Tennessee recover against the said George House the
sum of fifty dollars the amount of his recognizance in this
behalf acknowledged unless sufficient cause for such failure
be shewn -

State of Tennessee   )
Jno. Commins, Prosr.   )   T. A. B. on Prosecutor
    vs.   )
John Rymal   ) The Defendant who stands bound by
                    recognizance in the sum of one hundred
dollars for his appearance here to answer the State of Tennessee of a charge alledged against him for the commission of
an assault and battery on the body of John Commings was solemnly called for that purpose but came not and made default.
Therefore it is considered that the State of Tennessee recover
against the said John Rymal the sum of one hundred dollars
the amount of his recognizance in this behalf acknowledged
unless sufficient cause cause for such failure be shewn -
George House who stands bound by recognizance in the sum of
fifty dollars for the appearance here of John Rymal to answer
a charge of the State against him was solemnly called to
~~bring~~ bring into court the body of the said John Rymal was
surrender the Same in discharge of himself but failed so to
do whereupon it is considered that the State of Tennessee
recover against the said George House the sum of fifty dollars
the amount of his recognizance in this behalf acknowledged
unless sufficient cause for such failure be shewn   (P-211)

        Wednesday 24th. Jany. 1827.
The President, Directors and Company)
of the Bank of the State of Tennessee)   Debt
    vs.   )
Alexander Sevier, William K. Vance   )   This day came the
and Valentine Sevier   )   parties by attor-
                                          nies and thereupon
a jury to wit Jacob Carter, Samuel Bable, George Smith,
Daniel Carter Junr, Absalom Stonecypher, John Maloney Junr.

Christian Cook, Thomas Justice, Sparling Bowman, David Good, Lemuel Jones and Dalton Lane, who being elected tried and sworn the truth to speak upon the issue joined upon their oath do say that that the Defendants have not paid the Debt in the Declaration mentioned as in pleading they have alledged and they do assess the plaintiffs damages by reason of the detention of said debt to fifty one dollars and sixty cents - Therefore it is considered that the plaintiffs recover against the Defendants the sum of five hundred and nine dollars the debt in the declaration mentioned with the Damages by the jury aforesaid assessed and their costs by them about their suit in this behalf expended -

State of Tennessee)
Benedict Royal, prosr.)   Pettit Larceny
    vs.)
George Myers)   On motion and with the assent of
                     the court a nolliprosequi is
entered in this prosecution the costs of which was assumed by John Gass Junr. Benjamin Gregory and James Ross by Benjamin Gregory - Therefore it is considered by the Court that the State of Tennessee (P-212) recover against the said John Gass Junr. Benjamin Gregory and James Ross the costs aforesaid according to their assumpsit -

Martin Cline)
    vs.)   T. A. B.
William Houston)
                 Continued as on affidavit of plaintiff -

Wyly Craft)
    vs.)   Certio -
Jotham Brown Junr.)

                 This day came the parties by Attorney and thereupon a jury to wit Samuel Babb, George Smith, Daniel Carter Junr. Absalom Stonecypher, John Maloney, Christian Cook, Sparling Bowman, David Good, Lemuel Jones, Peter Couch and James Bell who being elected tried and sworn well and truly to try this cause upon their oath do say that they find for the plaintiff three dollars. Therefore it is considered that the plaintiff recover against the defendant and David Brown Security for the prosecution of his writ of Certiorari the aforesaid sum of three dollars and his costs by him about his suit in this behalf expended -

Daniel Allen executor)
of Hannah Baker Decd.)   Certiorari
    vs.)
Isaac Baker)   Continued on affidavit of Defendant

(P-213)   Wednesday 24th. January 1827.

Barbara Kirk for herself and)
as Guardian of the Minor)   Petition &c.
heirs of Joseph Kirk decd.)
     vs.)   This cause having come on
Joseph Davis)   to be heard and finally
                                      determined and the court
evidence being read to the Court because it appears to the
satisfaction of the court that the Defendant has in his
hands the amount of $185.35 of the estate of Joseph Kirk
decd. including interest to this time which he has not paid
It is therefore considered ordered adjudged and decreed by
the Court that the Defendant pay to the petitioner $185.35
together with the cost of this suit for which execution may
issue - From which judgment the Defendant by attorney prays
an appeal to the next circuit court of law to be held for
the County of Greene in the Courthouse in Greeneville on
the first Monday in March next - and having given bond and
security to prosecute his appeal is granted and the proceedings ordered to be certified -

Jacob T. Wyrick)
     vs.)   Certic
Andrew Park)
     The referees appointed to settle the
matters in desprate between the parties in this suit this
day made their award as followers - We after being sworn to
try a matter of despute existing between Jacob T. Wyrick and
Andrew Park and hearing all the evidence confirm and say
Lincolns judgment must stand together (P-214) with interest
amounting to thirty four dollars and ninety cents and that
said Park pay said Wyrick the amount thereof and that said
Wyrick pay all costs except Parks Attorneys fee also Parks
witnesses Wyrick is not to pay - Given under our hands &c.
24th. January 1827.

                            Moses G. Wilson
                            Thos. Murphy

     In confirmation whereof it is considered that the plain-
tiff recover against the defendant and Alexander Brown
Security for the prosecution of his writ of certiorari the
aforesaid sum of thirty four dollars and ninetycents and
that the Defendant recover against the plaintiff all the
costs of this suit except his own witnesses and the Attorneys Fee --

Michael Cobble   )
     vs.   )   Order Sale
Margaret Shannon, administratrix)
of the estate of Wm. Shannon decd.)   Leland Davis a
                                    constable of Greene
County returned here into court an execution issued by Hugh
Malony, esquire an acting justice of the peace for said
County against the estate of the Defendant for the sum of
Twenty two dollars and eighty seven cents debt and fifty
cents recovered by the plaintiff against the Defendant be-
fore said Justice on the 7th. day of November 1826 on which

execution said constable has made return "Search made and no personal property of the Defendant found and levied the execution on seven acres of land containing three islands on Chuckey River adjoining the lands of Hugh Malony and Allen Ragan & Clyme (P-215) Wednesday 24th. Jany. 1827 this 9th. day of November 1826.

Leland Davis Constable

Therefore on motion of the plaintiff by James W. Wyly his Attorney It is considered that the aforesaid seven acres of land so levied on be condemned to the satisfaction of the recovery aforesaid and that the same or so much thereof as well satisfy said recovery and the costs of this motion be sold as the law directs -

State of Tennessee)
    vs.)   Bastardy
Mary Keasling)

    The Defendant who stands bound by recognizance for her appearance here to indemnify the County of Greene in consequence of the Birth of a Bastard child of which she refuses to declare the father - Appeared according and entered into bond in the sum of six hundred dollars with Andrew Smiley Security continued that she shall perform such order as the court shall made from time to time concerning the maintainance of said child whereupon It is ordered that the said Mary Keasling pay the costs in this behalf expended and thereupon it is considered that the State of Tennessee recover against the said Andrew Smiley the costs aforesaid according to his assumpsit and also the Fine - (P-216)
$191.89

John M. Kilgore)
    vs.)   Motion for judgment for monies pd.
Thomas Cannon Admr.)   By Plaintiffs Security for Defdt.
of Wm. Kilgore Decd.)

    It appearing to the satisfaction of the Court that the plaintiff became security for William Kilgore in life time for a Debt due the Book of the State of Tennessee that in consequence of becoming security as aforesaid he has been compelled to pay the sum of one hundred ninety one dollars eighty nine cents.

    Therefore on motion of the plaintiff by James P. Taylor his attorney it is considered that the plaintiff recover of William Cannon administrator of the estate of William Kilgore decd. the aforesaid sum of $191.89 --- and the costs of this motion ----

John McKilgore)
    vs.)   Motion for Judgment against Defendant
Daniel Borden)   for monies paid as Co Security of Will-
                iam Kilgore Decd. -

    It appearing to the satisfaction of the Court that the plaintiff with the Defendants came securities for William Kilgore in his life time for a debt the Bank of the State of Tennessee that in consequence of becoming security as aforesaid he has been compelled to pay the sum of one hundred ninety one dollars and eighty nine cents - Therefore on motion of the plaintiff by James P. Taylor his attorney It is considered by the court that the plaintiff recover against the Defendant the sum of ninety five dollars ninety four and one half cents being the one (P-217) half of the amount of the aforesaid judgment and the costs of this motion

Samuel K. Gauntt,)
    vs.   ) Motion for Judgment for monies paid
Benedict Hoyal   )   also Security

        It appearing to the satisfaction of the Court that the plaintiff in consequence of becoming security with the Defendant in a debt due James M. Greenway assignee Jane Cochran has been compelled to pay the sum of eight dollars and forty cents. Therefore on motion of the plaintiff by John A. Aiken his Attorney It is considered that he recover against the Defendant the aforesaid sum of eight Dollars and forty cents and the costs of their motion -

Samuel K. Gauntt)
    vs.   ) Motion for Judgment for monies paid as
Frederick Young)   Co Security -

        It appearing to the satisfaction of the Court that the plaintiff in consequence of becoming security with the Defendant in a Debt due James M. Greenway assignee Jane Cochran has been compelled to pay the sum of five dollars thirty five and one half cents - Therefore on motion of the plaintiff by John A. Aiken his attorney -- It is considered that he recover against the Defendant the aforesaid sum of five dollars thirty five and one half cents and the costs of this motion -

    Grand and Pettit Jurors discharged 2 days
(P-218) Wednesday 24th. Jany. 1827

    And Court adjourned untill tomorrow morning 9 o'clock.
                      Jesse Kerby, J.P.
                      John Allison
                      Gilbert Woolsey

    Thursday 25th. Jany. 1827

    Court met Present:

    The Minutes of yesterdays proceedings were   and
      signed.

John Love)
    vs.   )   Certio Rule to Dismiss
George Wetty)

This day came the parties by attorney and thereupon
the rule entered to shew cause why the defendants petition
should be dismissed came on for argument - Whereupon all
and singular the premises being seen and by the court
fully understood - It is considered that said rule be
discharged -

And on motion of Defendant by Attorney writs of certiorari and supersedeas are awarded him returnable here
at next court (P-219) Thursday 25, Jany 1827.

Peter Parsons   )
    vs.   )   Ficre Facias
Robert Dickson, Administrator)
of Patrick O. Callaghan decd.)
                         In this cause a Fieri
                      Facias having been issued
and returned not satisfied except the sum of $46.75 and
that no personal property could be found to satisfy the
residue of the judgment in the hands of the administrator
has wasted the estate of his intestate - It is thereupon
considered and ordered by the court that a Scire Facias
issue against the said administrator commanding him to
appear at the next term of this court to shew cause why
the plaintiff should not have execution against the said
administrator to be levied of his own proper goods and
chattels lands and tenements for the residue of his Damages
and costs -

William Wilson   )
    vs.   )   Scire Facias
The Heirs at Law and)   Demurrer to Pleas
Children, of John   )
Russell, Decd.
                      By consent the Demurrer in this
                      cause to be argued at next court
and the issues submited to a jury -

John Baker   )
    vs.   )   T.VA.   Non Suit and Rule to set non suit
Peter Brown)   aside -

        This Day came the parties by Attornies and
thereupon the Rule entered to shew cause why (P-220)
the non suit suffered by the plaintiff should be set aside
came on for argument - Whereupon all and singular the
premises being seen and by the Court fully understood -
It is considered that said rule be made absolute -

State of Tennessee)
    vs.   )   Bastardy
Henry Engle   )
                      On motion of the Attorney General
ordered that a capias issue against the Defendant to Washington County.

State of Tennessee)
    vs.   )   Bastardy
James McKeehan   )

It appearing to the Court that a Bastardy fine has been incorrectly taxed to James McKeehan for the sum of $6.25. It is therefore ordered by the Court that said fine be released and that the Sheriff of Greene County have a credit on the books of the Trustee of Greene County for the amount of said fine -

Horace Rice   )
    vs.   )   Covt. Judg. Atthmt.
Thomas Falls   )

The plaintiff by his Attorney Peter Parsons esquire dismisses his suit and assumes the cost - Therefore it is considered by the court that the plaintiff pay the costs in this behalf expended -   (P-221) Thursday 25th
                                              Jany. 1827.

Aaron Finch   )
    vs.   )   The petition of the defendant was
James Phelps Senr.   )   presented by Robert McKenney his
                         Attorney praying writs of Certiorari
and Supersedeas upon consideration whereof It is ordered by the court that writs issue pursuant to the prayer of said petition returnable here at next court are the plaintiff giving bond and security according to Law -

Daniel M. Guin   )
    vs.   )   Scire Facias
David Farnsworth and   )   By Alfred Hunter, their Guardian -
Jane, his wife, Peter   )
R. Guin, Alfred Hunter)   Heirs and Devisees of the Real
and Elera his wife.   )   Estate of Robert Guin Decd. -
Alpha Guin &   )
Nancy Guin   )   This day came the plaintiff by
                              Attorney and the Scire Facias
issued in this cause being returned that the Defendants had acknowledged Service of the Same - and the said defendants not appearing nor do they say anything whereby the plaintiff remains against the said Defendants therein undefended - Therefore it is considered that the plaintiff's judgment in the writ of Scire Facias named be reminded and that the said Daniel M. Guin may have exception of his judgment and costs aforesaid heirs and Devisees and that the said   (P-222)   plaintiff recover against the heirs aforesaid his costs expended in sueing forthand prosecuting his writ of Scire Facias

And Court adjourned untill Court in Cause untill which time all matters and things in the same depending and undetermined are continued -
                                              Jesse Kerby, J.P.

(P-223)
State of Tennessee:
                         At a Court of Pleas and Quarter Sessions continued and held for the County of Greene in the Courthouse in Greeneville on the fourth Monday being the 23rd. day of April one thousand eight hundred and twenty seven was present

State of Tennessee)
     vs.   ) Bastary
Thomas Johnson   )

       The Defendant who stands bound by re-
cognizance for his appearance here to answer the State of
Tennessee of a charge alledged against him for begeting a
Bastard child of the body of Betsy Jones of this County
single woman appeared accordingly and entered into bond
in the sum of six hundred dollars with Joseph Johnson
Security conditioned that the said Thomas Johnson shall
perform such order as the court shall from time to time
make concerning the maintainance of said child - Whereupon
It is ordered that the said Thomas Johnson pay the costs
in this behalf expended - and thereupon Joseph Johnson
assumed for and on behalf of the said Thomas Johnson the
payment of the costs aforesaid and agrees that judgment be
entered against him for the same - Therefore it is considered
that the State of Tennessee recover against the said Joseph
Johnson the costs aforesaid according to his assumpsit -

(P-224) Monday 23rd. April 1827.

John Shanks   )
     vs.   ) Order Sale
James Davis Senr.)

       Turner Smith, a constable of Greene
County returned here into Court an execution issued by
Charles Bright esquire an acting justice of the peace for
said County against the estate of the defendant for the
sum of five dollars debt and one dollar cost recovered by
the plaintiff against the Defendant before said justice on
the 29th. day of December 1826 on which execution said
constable has made return - Search made and no goods or
chattels of James Davis Senr. found in my County - I have
levied this execution on four hundred acres of land in
two tracts or on all the interest and claim that the said
James Davis Senr. has to said four hundred acres in said
County on Main Lick Creek - adjoining the lands of Israel
Woolsey and myself levied on said land the 30th. of January
1827. by me, Turner Smith Const."
     Therefore on motion of the plaintiff by James P. Taylor
esquire his attorney. It is considered by the Court that
the aforesaid four hundred acres of land so levied on be
condemned to the satisfaction of the recovery aforesaid and
that the same or so much thereof as will satisfy said recovery and the costs of this motion be sold as the law directs -
     And Court adjourned untill tomorrow morning 9 o'clock.
                    A. Gillespie
                    Rankin
                    Frederick Smith

(P-225) Tuesday 24th. April 1827 Court sat present

     The Minutes of yesterday proceedings were read and
signed.

Thomas Holland)
  assignee &c.)   Certio
      vs.)
Jacob Garrett)   The plaintiff dismisses his suit and the
                   defendant assumes the payment of the costs.
Therefore it is considered that the plaintiff recover against
the defendant his costs in this suit -

Valentine Sevier Surviving   )
Partner of Deaderick &   ) Covenant
Sevier for the use of Alexander)
Anderson   ) The plaintiff dismisses
     vs.   ) his suit and assumes the
John Guin and Daniel Guin   ) payment of the taxed of
                       the costs. Therefore it
is considered that parties recover against each other the
costs aforesaid according to their assumpsits -

William Brown)
    vs.)   Certio
Isaac Jones)
        On motion of Michael Bright Security of
Isaac Jones in this suit a Rule is allowed him to (P-226)
shew cause why the tax above of the costs in this suit as
respects the witnesses attendance and the constable charge
of $7.65 should be corrected.

William M. P. Mitchell)
    vs.)   Certio
John Graham)
        On motion of plaintiff by attorney
a Rule is allowed him to shew cause why the Defendants petition
and writ should be dismissed
    And by leave of the Court the judgment given in this
cause is filed by the justice who gave the same -

George Walter)
    vs.)   Debt
James Allen)
        The Defendant by his written agreement con-
fesses judgment according to specialty - Therefore it is considered that the plaintiff recover against the defendant the
sum of two hundred and twelve dollars and thirty two cents
the amount of the specialties declared onand his costs by
him about his suit in this behalf expended -
    And the Plaintiff by Attorney Stays execution nine months.

William Alexander)
    vs.)   Certio
John Light)
        The petition of the Defendant was presented
by James W. Wyly his Attorney praying Writs of Certiorari and
Supersedeas - Upon consideration whereof It is ordered that
writs issue pursuant to the prayer of said petition on Bond
and Security being given according to Law

(P-227)   Tuesday 24th. April 1827.

Richard M. Woods esquire high Sheriff in and for the
County of Greene returns here into open court the States
writ of Venire Facias to him directed endorsed "Returnable
Tuesday after the fourth Monday in April 1827 Issd. 5th.
February 1827 " Recd. 6th. Feby. executed on all but Samuel Ellis, George Kennedy, John Ketching and Jas. Rutherford ."

R. M. Woods Sheriff

Out of whom are selected as the Statutes in that case prov-
ides the following Gentleman a grand, Inquest and Jury
Adam Dunwoody appointed Foreman by Court James McCloughan,
William Crabtree, Thomas Mitchell, William Brown David Good,
Moses Shanks, Robert Russell, John Peak, Clairborne Jones,
Andrew Davis, Omasa Harrold, Peter Lekins, good and lawful
men of the County of Greene aforesaid who being now here
empannelled and sworn in the Courthouse in Greeneville to
enquire for the State aforesaid and for the Body of the
County of Greene aforesaid received their charge and retired
from the Bar.

Andrew McPherran, a constable was qualified to attend
on the above jury 4 days.

On motion and for reasons shewn ordered that Vincent
Jackson, Jacob Misner, William Hall, Christopher Havn and
Reubin Murray be severally discharged from further attend-
ance of the present court as Jurors --

Turner Smith, a constable to attend on the court -
4 days certificate issd.

(P-228)   Tuesday 24th. April 1827.

Christian Dyche, the residue of the Venire to the
present court is to attend the same as a pettit juror
untill discharged.

John Moyers   )
     vs.   )   Order Sale
James Thompson)

William Barkley, a constable of Greene
County returned here into court an execution issued by John
Matthews esquire an acting justice of the peace for said
County against the estate of the defendant for the sum of
eight dollars sixty two and one half cents debt and the
further sum of one dollar and fifty cents cost recovered
by the plaintiff against the defendant before said justice
on the 17th. day of February 1827 on which execution said
constable has made return made search no goods & chattels
to be found in my county levied the within execution on the
23rd. April 1827 on one tract of land containing sixty acres
or upward and one tract of thirty acres joining the lands
of Moses Reese, John Reese, and David Stanfield on the
waters of Sinking creek, William Barkley constable.

Therefore on motion of the plaintiff by James P.
Taylor his attorney it is considered that the aforesaid
two tracts of land so levied on be condemned to the satisfaction of the recovery aforesaid and that the same or so
much thereof as will satisfy said recovery and the costs
of this motion be sold as the law directs. -

Washington Henshaw one of)
the executors of Absalom)   Order Sale
Haworth decd.)
    vs.)   William Barkley, a constable
James Thompson)   of (P-229) Greene County
                      returned here into Court an
execution issued by John Matthews esquire an acting justice
of the peace for said County against the estate of the defendant for the sum of thirty six dollars ninety five cents
Debt and one dollar and fifty cents cost recovered by the
plaintiff against the defendant before said justice on the
17th. day of February 1827 - on which execution said constable
has made return made seach no goods and chattels to be found
in my county levied the within execution 23rd. April 1827
on one tract thirty acres joining each other, joining the
lands of Moses Reese, John Reese, and David Stanfield on
the water of sinking creek. William Barkley constable.
    Therefore on motion of the plaintiff by James P. Tay-
lor his attorney it is considered that the aforesaid two
tracts of land so levied on be condemned to the satisfaction of the of the recovery aforesaid and that the same or
so much thereof as will satisfy said recoveryand the costs
of this motion be sold as the law directs -

David Waddle for J. & A. Prestons use)
    vs.)   Covt.
Thomas Holland)
                  The Defendant in his
proper person comes into court and confesses judgment for the
sum of sixty six dollars sixty six and two thirds cents with
interest thereon from the twenty fifth of December 1825 amounting in the whole to the sum of seventy two dollars. Therefore it is considered that the plaintiff recover against
the Defendant the aforesaid sum of seventy two dollars and
his costs by him about his suit in this behalf expended -
(P-230) Tuesday 24th. April 1827. And Court adjourned
untill tomorrow morning 9 o'clock.
                    A. Gillespie
                    Lewis Ball
                    Thomas Murphy

Wednesday 25th. April 1827

Court met present

The Minutes of yesterdays proceedings were read and
signed. --

State of Tennessee)
John Cummings, Prosr.)   T. A. B.
    vs.)
John Rimal)   On motion and with the assent of
                     the Court a Nolli Prosequi is
entered in this prosecution the costs of which are ordered
to be paid by the Defendant and thereupon George House
assumed for and on behalf of the Defendant the payment
of the costs aforesaid and agrees that judgment be entered
against him for the same - Therefore it is considered that
the State of Tennessee recover against the said George House
the costs aforesaid according to his assumpsit -

State of Tennessee)
John Cummings, Prosr.)   T. A. B.
    vs.)
John Rimal)   On motion and with the assent
           (P-231) of the Court a Nolli
Prosequi is entered in this prosecution the costs of which
an order to be paid by the defendant and thereupon George
House assumed for and on behalf of the defendant the pay-
ment of the costs aforesaid and agree that judgment be
entered against him for the same - Therefore the said
George House the costs aforesaid to his assumpsit -

State of Tennessee)
    vs.)   Sci Fa. Recog.
John Rimel)
           On motion and with the consent of the
consent of the court the forfeiture in this writ of Scire
Facias named is set aside the cost whereof is ordered to
be paid by the Defendant the payment of the costs aforesaid
and agrees that judgment be entered against the said George
House the cost aforesaid according to his assumpsit -

State of Tennessee)
    vs.)   Sci Fa. Forft. Recog.
John Rimel)
          On motion and with the assent of the
Court the forfeiture in this writ of Scire Facias named is
set aside the costs whereof is ordered to be paid by the
defendant - and thereupon George House assumed for and behalf of the Defendant the payment of the costs aforesaid
and agrees that judgment be entered against him for the
same.
    Therefore it is considered that the State of Tennessee
recover against the said George House the payment of the
costs aforesaid according to his assumpsit - (P-232)
               Wednesday 25th. April 1827.
State of Tennessee)
    vs.)   Sci Fa. Foftd. Recog.
George House Bail)
of John Rimel)   On motion and with the assent of the
             assent of the Court the forfeiture in
this writ of Scire Facias named is set aside and the costs

assumed by the defendant.

Therefore it is considered that the State of Tennessee recover against the said George House the costs aforesaid according to his assumpsit -

State of Tennessee)
    vs.)   Sci Fa. Forftd. Recog.
George House bail)
of John Rimel)   On motion and with the assent of
    the Court the forfeiture in this

writ of Scire Facias named is set aside and the costs of the same assumed by the defendant. Therefore it is considered that the State of Tennessee recover against the said George House, the costs aforesaid according to his assumpsit -

Robert Patterson)
    vs.)   Certio
David E. W. Bable &)
Jacob Newman)   The plaintiff dismisses his suit
    and the Defendants assume the pay-

ments of the costs - Therefore it is considered that the plaintiff recover against the defendants his costs by him about his suit in this behalf expended -

(P-233)   Wednesday 25th. April 1827
State of Tennessee)
    vs.)   Recognized &c.
Thomas Jackson)
    On motion and with the assent of the

Court Nolli Prosequi is entered in this prosecution and the Defendant ordered to be discharged -

State of Tennessee)
Alexander Caldwell Prosr.)   T. A. B. & Riot
    vs.)
Henry Monteeth Junr.)   This day came as well the Attor-
    ney General as the Defendant in

his proper person and the defendant being charged on the Bill of Indictment for plea says that he is guilty in manner and form as charged in the Bill of Indictment and puts himself on the mercy of the Court. Therefore it is considered that the Defendant for such his offence be fined forfeiture and pay to the State of Tennessee the sum of twenty five cents and that he pay the costs of this prosecution -

And therefore came XXXXX Nicholas Shanks and assumed for and on behalf of the Defendant the payment of the fine and costs aforesaid and agrees that judgment be entered against him for the Same - Therefore it is considered that the State of Tennessee recover against the said Nicholas Shanks the Fine and costs aforesaid according to his Suit -

State of Tennessee)
Bryant Deaton Prosr.)   T. A. B.
    vs.)
James Johnson)   This day came as well the Attorney

General as the Defendant in his proper person and the Defendant (P-234) being charged on the Bill of Indictment for plea thereto says that he is not guilty in manner and form as charged in the Bill of Indictment and puts himself on the Country and the Attorney General having done the like came also a jury to wit, Christian Dyche, David Logan, Nicholas Shanks, Nathan Hoggatt, Henry Garrett, James Moore, Henry Montgeth, James Shanks, William Thomason, William M. P. Mitchell, Ironymus Dyche, and Aaron Mills who being elected tried and sworn the truth to speak upon this issue of Traverse upon their oath do say that the Defendant is guilty in manner and form as charged in the Bill of Indictment.

Therefore it is considered that the Defendant for such his offence be fined, forfeit, and pay to the State of Tennessee the sum of one dollar and that he pay the costs of this prosecution -

State of Tennessee)
Howell Houston, Prosr.) T. A. B. on Jas. Horten
   vs.)
Samuel Allen) This day came as well the Attorney
General as the Defendant in his proper person and the Defendant being charged on the Bill of Indictment for plea thereto say that he is guilty in manner and form as charged in the Bill of Indictment and puts himself on the mercy of the court. Therefore it is considered that the Defendant for such his offence be fined forfeit and pay to the State of Tennessee the sum of one dollar and that he pay the costs of this prosecution -

State of Tennessee)
   vs.) Sci Fa. Forftd. Recog.
Ira Green)
On motion and with the assent (P-235) of the Court ordered that the forfeiture in this writ of Scire Facias named be set aside and that the costs of the same be paid by the Defendant and thereupon the said Ira Green assumed that the State of Tennessee recover against the said Ira Greene the costs aforesaid according to his assumpsit -

State of Tennessee)
   vs.) Sci Fa. Forftd. Recog.
Ira Green)
On motion and with the assent of the Court ordered that the forfeiture in this writ of Scire Facias named be set aside on the payment of the costs of the same which are assumed by the said Ira Green.

Therefore it is considered that the State of Tennessee recover against the said Ira Green the costs aforesaid according to his assumpsit -

Isaac Humbard)
   vs.) Certio
James Hise)

On motion of plaintiff by Attorney a Rule is allowed him to shew cause why the Defendants petition and writ should be dismissed -

Daniel Casteel)
      vs.   ) Certio
Omy Malone   )

                Continued by consent

Same   )
vs.   ) Certio
Daniel Casteel)

                Continued as on affidavit plaintiff.

(P-236)   Wednesday 25th. April 1827.
State of Tennessee)
      vs.   )   Bastardy
Hiram Engle   )

                On motion and with the assent of the Court a Nolli Prosequi is entered in this prosecution and the costs ordered to be paid by the defendant. Therefore it is considered that the State of Tennessee recover against the said Hiram Engle the costs aforesaid -

State of Tennessee)
  Ira Greene Prosr.)   Continued as on affidavit of Defend-
      vs.   )   ant Jacob Hise acknowledged to owe
Jacob Hise   )   the State of Tennessee one hundred
                        Dollars and James Hise his surety
also acknowledged to owe the State of Tennessee the sum of one hundred dollars - Yet upon condition that if Jacob Hise shall make his personal appearance at the Court of Pleas and Quarter Sessions to be held for the County of Greene in the Courthouse in Greeneville on Wednesday next after the fourth Monday in July next and stand his trial in the above prosecution against him and not depart the court of pleas and quarter Sessions to be held for the County of Green in the Courthouse in Greeneville on Wednesday next after the fourth Monday in July next and prosecute and give evidence on behalf of the State of Tennessee against Jacob Hise and not depart the court without leave this recognizance to be void otherwise in force. -
(P-237) Wednesday 25th. April 1827.

State of Tennessee   )
Bryant Deaton, Prosecutor)   T. A. B.
  vs.   )
Peter Brown   )   This day came as well the
                              Attorney General as the
Defendant in his proper person and the Defendant being charged on the Bill of Indictment for plea thereto say that he is not guilty in manner and form as charged in the Bill of Indictment and puts himself on the Country and the Attorney General having done the like came also

a Jury to wit Thomas Lawson, James Lackland, Michael
Boysinger, John Parsons, Thorton Hendry, Emanuel Parman,
David Brumley, Jacob Carter, John Delashmit, Frederick
Young, John Hoyal, and Jesse Reynolds who being elected
tried and sworn the truth to speak upon this issue of
traverse upon their oath do say that the Defendant is
guilty in manner and form as charged in the Bill of Indictment. Therefore it is considered that the Defendant for
such his offence be fined forfeit and pay to the State of
Tennessee the sum of twenty five cents and the costs of this
prosecution Rule for new Trial discharged from the judgment
residued in this prosecution the defendant by Attorney prays
an appeal to the next circuit court of Greene County to be
held in the next circuit court of Greene County to be held
in the Courthouse in Greeneville on the first Monday in
September next which appeal is granted and the proceedings
ordered to be certified and thereupon Peter Brown acknowledged to owe to the State of Tennessee Two Hundred and
fifty dollars and Tilman A. Howard his security also acknowledge to owe the State of Tennessee Two hundred and fifty
dollars yet upon condition that if Peter Brown shall make
his personal appearance at the Circuit Court of Law to be
held for the County of Greene in the Courthouse in Greeneville on Tuesday next after the first Monday in September
next after the first Monday in September next and stand
his trial (P-238) in this prosecution against him and
not depart the Court without leave the above recognizance
to be void otherwise in force - and thereupon Bryant Deaton
the prosecutor acknowledged to owe to the State of Tennessee
the sum of Two hundred dollars yet to be void on condition
that he shall make his personal appearance at the Circuit
Court of Law to be held for the County of Greene in the
Courthouse in Greeneville on Tuesday next after the first
Monday in September next and prosecute and give evidence
on behalf of the State of Tennessee in this prosecution
against Peter Brown and not depart the court without leave
then the above recognizance to be void otherwise in force -

State of Tennessee   )
Andrew Caldwell, prosr.)   T. A. B. & Riot
   vs.   )
James Shanks   )   This day came as well the Attor-
                               ney General as the Defendant in
his proper person and the Defendant being charged on the
Bill of Indictment for plea thereto says that he is not
guilty in manner and form as therein against him is alledged
and puts himself on the Country and the Attorney General
having done the same also a jury to wit Amos McBride,
Henry Henegar, James Johnson, Andrew Stephens, Samuel Allen,
Allen Rose, Henry Freshour, John Baker, William Buster,
Samuel McKeehan, Amyntas A. Ortto and William Blair who
being elected tried and sworn well and truly to try this
issue of Traverse upon their oath do say that the Defendant
is guilty in manner and form as charged in the Bill of Indictment Therefore it is considered that the Defendant for such

his offence be fined forfeit and pay to the State of Tennessee the sum of one cent and that he pay the costs of (P-239) this prosecution and thereupon came Nicholas Shanks and assumed for and on behalf of the Defendant the payment of the Fine and cost aforesaid and agrees that judgment be entered against him for the same - Therefore it is considered that the State of Tennessee recover against the said Nicholas Shanks the fine and costs aforesaid to his assumpsit -

State of Tennessee)
William Thomason Prosr.)   T. A. B.
    vs.   )
Nathan Hoggatt   )   This day came as well the Attorney General as the Defendant in his proper person and the Defendant being charged on the Bill of Indictment for plea thereto says that he is not guilty in manner and form as therein against him is alledged and puts himself on the Country and the Attorney General having done the same came also a jury to wit, Christian Dyche, Nicholas Shanks, Henry Garrett, James Shanks, William M. P. Mitchell, Ironymus Dyche, Aaron Mills, Marmaduke Lamb John Baker, Richard West, Jeremiah Casteel and Martin Cline who being elected tried and sworn the truth to speak upon this issue of Traverse upon their oath do say that the Defendant is guilty in manner and form as charged in the Bill of Indictment -

Therefore it is considered that the defendant for such his offence be fined forfeit and pay to the State of Tennessee the sum of one dollar and that he pay the costs of this prosecution -

State of Tennessee) Andrew Caldwell, Prosr.
    vs.   ) This day came as well (P-240) Attorney General as the Defendant in his
Andrew Shanks   ) proper person and the Defendant being charged on the Bill of Indictment for plea thereto says that he is guilty in manner and form as therein against him is alledged and puts himself on the mercy of the Court therefore it is considered that the Defendant for such his offence be fined forfeit and pay to the State of Tennessee one cent and thereupon Nicholas Shanks in his proper person appeared in court and assumed for and on behalf of the Defendant the payment of the fine and costs aforesaid and agrees that judgment be entered against him for the same therefore it is considered that the State of Tennessee Recover against the said Nicholas Shanks the fine and cost aforesaid according to his Assumpsit -

State of Tennessee   )
Andrew Caldwell, Pros.)   T. A. B. & Riot
    vs.   )
Moses Shanks, a Minor)   Continued as on Affidavit Defendant and thereupon Nicholas Shanks

acknowledged to owe the State of Tennessee the sum of one
hundred dollars yet upon condition that if Moses Shanks a
minor shall make his personal appearance at the Court of
pleas and quarter sessions to be held for the County of
Greene in the Court house in Greeneville on Wednesday next
after the fourth Monday in July next and stand his trial
in this prosecution against him and not depart the court
without leave then the above recognizance to be void otherwise in force Andrew Caldwell also acknowledged to owe the
State of Tennessee one hundred dollars yet upon conditions
that if he shall make his personal appearance at the court
of pleas and quarter sessions to be held for (P-241) the
County of Greene in the Courthouse in Greeneville on Wednesday next after the fourth Monday in July next and prosecute
and give evidence on behalf of the State of Tennessee against
Moses Shanks and not depart the court without leave then this
recognizance to be void otherwise in force -

George Alexander   )
    vs.   )   Certio
Andrew Howell   )
                The petition of the Defendant was
presented by James W. Wyly his Attorney praying writs of
certiorari and supersedeas upon condition whereof it is
ordered that writs issue pursuant to the prayer of said
petition on Bond and Security being given according to Law.

William Dickson   )
agent for Hugh Murray   )   Certio
    vs.   )
Abner Williams   )   The petition of the plaintiff
                   was presented by James W. Wyly
his Attorney praying writs of Certiorari and Supersedeas -
Upon consideration whereof it is ordered that writs issue
pursuant to the prayer of said petition upon Bond and Security being given according to Law -

     And Court adjourned untill tomorrow morning 9 o'clock.
                            Henry Dyche
                            Thomas Murphey
                            Hugh Maloney
(P-242) Thursday 26th. April 1827.

     The Minutes of yesterdays proceedings were read and
signed.

Merryman Payne   )
  Assignee John Baker)   Certio
    vs.   )
James Baker   )   The Defendant by his attorney
                    confesses that he owes the plain-
tiff the sum of seventy five dollars with interest thereon
from the 8th. January one thousand eight hundred and twenty
two amounting to the sum of twenty three dollars eighty four

and one half cents -

Therefore it is considered that the plaintiff recover against the said Defendant and John Gladen and Howell Houston securities for the prosecution of the Defendants writ of Certiorari the aforesaid sum of ninety eighty dollars eighty four and one half cents the debt and interest aforesaid and his costs by him about his suit in this behalf expended -

Alexander Anderson Assignee)
David Deaderick & Son   ) Debt
    vs.   )
George Brown   ) The Defendant confesses judgment for the Sum of one hundred forty seven dollars and sixty six cents the residue of the Debt and Interest in the Declaration mentioned - Therefore it is considered that the plaintiff recover against the Defendant the aforesaid sum of one hundred forty seven dollars and (P-245) Sixty Six cents and his costs by him about his suit in this behalf expended -

                    Execution staid 3 months -

(P-244)   Thursday 26th. April 1827.
Elisha Moore   )
    vs.   ) Covenant
James Allen   )

      The Defendant by his attorney confesses judgment for the sum of one hundred and thirty two dollars and seventy five cents - Therefore it is considered that the plaintiff recover against the Defendant the aforesaid sum of one hundred thirty two dollars and seventy five cents and his costs by him about his suit in this behalf expended -
                    Execution staid 3 months -

Richard Clevenger for)
John Wood's use   ) Covenant
    vs.   )
James Allen   ) The Defendant by his attorney confesses judgment for the sum of four hundred and eight dollars and nine cents.

Therefore it is considered that the plaintiff recover against the Defendant the aforesaid sum of four hundred and eight dollars and nine cents and his costs by him about his suit in this behalf expended -

                    Execution staid 3 months.

Jacob Hornbarger)
    vs.   ) Debt Specie
James Galbreath   )

      This day came the parties by Attornies and thereupon a jury to wit Peter Likens, Christian Dyche, William Pearce, David Logan, Amos McBride, William M. P. Mitchell, Henegar, Andrew McPherson, Jacob Hull, John Baker Samuel Bridewell and Marmaduke Lamb who being elected tried and sworn well and truly to try this cause upon their oath do say that the defendant (P-245) has not paid the Debt in the Declaration mentioned as in pleading he hath alledged and assess the plaintiffs Damages by reason of the detention of that Debt to forty dollars and eighty seven cents. Therefore it is considered that the plaintiff recover against the Defendant the sum of one hundred and fifty six dollars (in Spicie) the Debt in the declaration mentioned with the Damages by the jury aforesaid assessed and his costs by him about his Suit in this behalf expended -

Adam Pitner)
   vs.   ) Case
James Allen)

   This day came the Defendant by Attorney and the plaintiff although solemnly called came not neither is his suit prosecuted. Therefore it is considered that the plaintiff be non pros and that the Defendant recover against the plaintiff his his costs by him about his defence in this behalf expended -

The Heirs of John)
   Russell Decd.) Covent.
     vs.   )
Samuel Bridewell) Continued as on affidavit of Defendant

John Baker)
   vs.   ) T. V. A.
Peter Brown)

   This day came the parties by Attornies and thereupon a jury to wit James McCloughan, Thomas Mitchell Junr. David Good, Adam Dunwoody, Robert Russell, Claiborne Jones, Omasa Harrold (P-246) William Crabtree, William Brown, Moses Shanks, John Peak, and Andrew Davis who being elected tried and sworn well and truly to try this cause upon their oath do say that the Defendant is not guilty of the Trespass in the plaintiffs declaration mentioned.
   Therefore it is considered that the plaintiff take nothing by his suit and that the Defendant recover against the plaintiff his costs by him about his defence in this behalf expended-

John Love)
   vs.   ) Certiorari
George Wetty)

   The Defendant having filed his petition and obtained an order for writs of certiorari and supersedeas and having failed to prosecute his said writ It is ordered by the court that said petition be quashed and that the plaintiff recover against the Defendant and John M. Kilgore and John Walker securities for the prosecution of the Defendants writ of certiorari his costs by him about his suit in this behalf -
   And on motion of the plaintiff by attorney a procedendo is awarded him directed to Henry Dyche esquire the justice who gave judgment in this cause -

Robert I. McKinney)
    vs.   )   Order Sale
John Baker   )

      James Britton Junr. a constable of
Greene County returned here into court an execution issued
by Joseph Brown esquire an acting justice of the peace for
said County against the estate of the Defendant for the sum
of five dollars and thirty one cents debt recovered by the
plaintiff against the   (P-247)   Defendant before said
justice on the 26th. day of April 1827, on which execution
said constable has made return "Search made and no property
found in my County claimed by defendant therefore levied on
all the right title, claim and interest that John Baker has
of in and to an undivided tract of land of 67½ acres of land
lying on Chuckey River joining John Kifer, and one entry of
Alexander Hall, and also joining an entry of Peter Brown –
this 26th. April 1827 –
                       Jas. Britton, Const.
    Therefore on motion – It is considered that all the right
title, claim and interest of the said John Baker of in and
to the aforesaid tract of land be condemned to the satisfaction of the recovery aforesaid&that the same or so much thereof as will satisfy said recovery and the costs of this motion
be sold as the law directs –

Martin Cline   )
    vs.   )   T. V. A.
William Houston)

      This day came the parties by attornies
and thereupon a jury to wit Peter Likens, Christian Dyche,
William Pearce, David Logan, Omas McBride, William M. P.
Mitchell, Henry Henegar, Andrew McPherson, Jacob Hull, John
Baker, Samuel Bridewell, Marmaduke Lamb, who being elected
tried and sworn well and truly to try this cause upon the
Trespass in manner and form as the plaintiff against him in
his Declaration hath complained Therefore it is considered
that the plaintiff take nothing by his suit and that the
Defendant recover against the plaintiff his costs by him about
his defence in this behalf expended – (P-248)

Thursday 26th. April 1827.
John Balch   )
  vs.   )   Certio
James McPherson)

      This day came the parties by attornies and
thereupon a jury to wit John Hoyal, Martin Bailey, John English, Abraham C. Fellers, William Brannon, William Standfield
Jacob Smith, Nathan Carter, Hezekiah B. Gass, William Stanley,
Frederick Young, Thomas Davis Junr. who being elected tried
and sworn well and truly to try this cause retained to the
bar and declared they could not agree –
    During the progress of this suit William Barkley summoned
to give evidence on behalf of the Defendant was solemnly
called for that purpose but came.

Therefore it is considered that the said William
Barkley forfeit and pay to the use of Defendant the sum of
one hundred and twenty five dollars pursuant to act of
assembly unless sufficient cause for such failure be shewn -
And Court adjourned untill tomorrow morning 9 o'clock

Joseph Brown, J.P.
R. Maloney, J.P
John Balch, J.P
C. Dyche, J.P

(P-249) Friday 27th. April 1827.

Court met present

The Minutes of yesterdays proceedings were read and
signed -

Henry Henegar   )
    vs.   ) Attachment
Thomas Davis   )

         Rule to declare so as not to delay

Simmons Crawford   )
Administrator Jesse Winfrey Decd.   ) Attachment
    vs.   )
Jonathan Wood   ) Rule to declare so as
                                   not to delay

Isaac Humbard)
    vs.   ) Certio Rule to dismiss
James Hise   )

        This day came the parties by attornies and
thereupon the Rule entered to shew cause why the Defendants
petition and writ should be dismissed came on for argument.
       Whereupon all and singular the premises being seen and
by the Court fully understood it is considered that said rule
be made absolute and that the plaintiff recover against the
Defendant and William Standfield Security for the prosecution
of the defendants writ of certiorari the sum of ninety three
dollars and fifteen cents the debt recovered before the justice
with 12½ pr. cent thereon from the 4th. October 1826 and his
costs by him about his suit in this (P-250) _in this_ behalf
expended -

William M. P. Mitchell)
    vs.   ) Certio Rule to dismiss
John Graham   )

        This day came the parties by attor-
nies and thereupon the rule entered to shew cause why the
defendants petition and writ should be dismissed came on for
argument whereupon all and singular the premises being seen
and by the court fully understood. It is considered that
said Rule be discharged.

Daniel Allen executor)
of Hannah Baker, decd.)   Certio
    vs.   )
Isaac Baker   )   On motion and cause shewn by
                       affidavit of Howell Houston
this cause is continued untill the next term of this court.

Samuel Jackson, assignee)
  John A. Aiken   )   Covenant
    vs.   )
Howell Houston   )   This day came the parties by
                       Attornies and thereupon a
jury to wit James Mc.Clougher, Thomas Mitchell, David
Good, Adam Dunwoody, Robert Russell, Claiborne Jones, Omasa
Harrold, William Crabtree, William Brown, Moses Shanks,
John Reah and Andrew Davis who being elected tried and sworn
well and truly to try this cause upon their oath do say that
the Defendant has not kept and performed his covenant as in
pleading he hath alledged but has broken the same in manner
and form as the plaintiff against him hath alledged (P-251)
and they do assess the plaintiffs damages by occasion thereof
to one hundred and Two Dollars thirty seven and one half
cents - Therefore it is considered that the plaintiff recover
against the Defendant the Damages aforesaid by the jury aforesaid assessed and his costs by him about his suit in this
behalf expended -

      Grand and Pettit Jurors discharged 4 days

William Wilson   )
   vs.   ) Scire Facias
The Heirs at Law and   )
Children of John Russell, Decd.) Continued by consent untill
                          next Court - and should
John Kennedy or John A. McKinney be absent to be continued
untill October Court.

James McPherson)
   vs.   ) Certio Rule to dismiss
James Gibson   )
               This day came the parties by attornies
and thereupon the rule entered to shew cause why the Defendants petition and writ should be dismissed came on for argument whereupon all and singular the premises being seen and
by the Court fully understood - It is considered that said
Rule be discharged -

Andrew Davis)
   vs.   ) Certio
Philip Harmon)
               The petition of the Defendant was presented
by John A. Aiken his Attorney (P-252) praying writs of
certiorari and supersedeas upon consideration whereof it is
ordered that said petition be granted and that writs issue
pursuant to the prayer of the same on bond and security being
given according to law.

Henry Earnest)
  vs.)   Debt Atthmt.
James Thompson)

      This day came the plaintiffs by attorney
and the Defendant although solemnly called came not but made
default. Therefore it is considered that the plaintiff
recover against the Defendant the sum of one hundred twenty
five dollars fifty two ½ cents the residue of the debt and
interest in the declaration mentioned and his costs by
him about his suit in this behalf expended -

William Dickson for)
Alexander Williams use)   Debt
  vs.)
David L. Swain, administrator)   This day came the parties
of Robert Nelson decd.)   by attornies and thereupon
                            a jury to wit James McClogher
Thomas Mitchell, David Good, Adam Dunwoody, Robert Russell,
Claiborne Jones, Omasa Harrold, William Crabtree, William
Brown, Moses Shanks, John Reah, and Andrew Davis who being
elected tried and sworn well and truly to try this cause upon
their oath do say that the said Defendant David L. Swain hath
fully administrated all and singular the goods and chattels
which were of Robert Nelson deceased at the time of his death
and which had come to his hands to be administered at the
time of instituting this (P-253) Suit as in pleading he hath
alledged - Therefore it is considered that the plaintiff
recover the sum of five hundred and twenty eight dollars and
fifteen cents the plaintiffs debt in the declaration mentioned
with the further sum of one hundred and thirty nine dollars
for interest due and accrued thereon to be levied of the goods
and chattels of the intestate when assent sufficient shall
come to the Defendants hands to be administrated.
      And it being now suggested to the court that the said
Robert Nelson died seized and possessed of real estate with-
in the State of Tennessee which decended to Charles Neilson
Archibald D. Neilson, Sarah L. Neilson, James R. Garrett, and
Jane his wife formerly Jane Neilson, Joseph S. Chun and
Catharine his wife, formely Catherine Neilson, Philip Neilson
(Elizabeth D. Neilson) Robert Strong, Charles Reedy, and
Martha his wife formely Martha Strong, Joseph Strong, Green
R. Cesna, George Gillespie and Anna his wife formely Anna
Neilson - Therefore on motion of the plaintiff a Scire
Facias is awarded him against the real estate of the said
Robert Nelson decd. should not issue pursuant to act of
assembly -

Aaron Finch)
  vs.)   Certio
James Felts)

      This day came the plaintiff by Attorney and
the Defendant although solemnly called came not but made
default - Therefore it is considered by the court that the
plaintiff recover against the Defendant the sum of twenty

five dollars with interest thereon from the 26th. July 1826
and his costs by him about his suit in this behalf expended -
(P-254) Friday 27th. April 1827

Summon Crawford Administrator)
of Jesse Winfrey Decd.   )   Attachment
        vs.   )
Jonathan Woods   )   This day came the plaintiff
                                       by attorney and James Allen
who had been summoned as Gurdishee by the Sheriff to answer
on oath what of the goods and chattels or effects of Jonathan
Woods he has in his hands was solemnly called for the purpose
but came not - Therefore it is considered that the plaintiff
recover against the said James Allen Garnishee as aforesaid
the sum of two thousand one hundred and ninety eight dollars
the amount of the plaintiffs claim against the Defendant
according to his complaint and his costs - And on motion of
the plaintiff by Attorney a Scire Facias is awarded him against
the said James Allen returnable here at our next court to shew
cause if any he hath why final judgment should not be entered
against him for amount of the plaintiff claim - and costs.

(P-255) Blank.
(P-256)

State of Tennessee
        Be it remembered that at a court of pleas and quarter
sessions continued and held for the County of Greene in the
Court House in Greeneville on the fourth Monday (being the
23rd. day of July 1827)
                    was present -

David Kelly   )
    vs.   )   Wards
Hiram Engledow)
        The plaintiff in his proper person dismisses
his suit and the Defendant assumes the payment of the costs.
Therefore it is considered that the plaintiff recover against
the Defendant his costs in this behalf expended -
        And Court adjourned untill tomorrow morning 10 o'clock
                            M. Lincoln J.P.
                            Cornelius Smith J.P.
                            Isaac Justice J.P.

        Tuesday 24th. July 1827
        Court met present The Minutes of yesterdays proceedings
were read and signed -

(P-257) Tuesday 24th. July 1827
        Richard M. Woods esquire high sheriff in and for the
County of Greene returns here into open court the States writ
of Venire Facias to him directed endorsed "Returnable Tuesday
after the 4th. Monday in July 1827 Issd. 10th. May 1827 executed
on all but Thomas Magill, John McMackin.
                            R.M. Woods Shff.

·Out of whom are selected as the Statutes in that case
provides the following gentlemen a grand inquest and jury
to wit:

Alfred Glascock appointed Foreman by the Court

Eliakim Cox	Joseph Hurley
William Reader	John T. Vestal
John Stine	John Lady
James Lackland	James H. McFarland
Obodiah Light	John Harrison
James Scott	John Laughner

good and lawful men of the County of Greene aforesaid who
being now here empannelled and sworn in the courthouse in
Greeneville to enquire for the State aforesaid and for the
body of the County of Greene aforesaid received their charge
and returned from the Bar James Gass, Constable was qualified
to attend on the above jury 3 days certifed. issd.

On motion and for reasons disclosed ordered that George
Jackson, James Shields, John Harman, Michael, George Allen
Ross, Thomas Eolland and Willis Gray be released from further
attendance as jurors at the present court -

Wyatt Hill, John Craig, John Love and John Hunter the residue of the Venire to the present court are to attend the
same as pettit jurors respectively untill discharged -

Turner Smith constable to attend on the court
4 days certifed issd.

(P-258)   Tuesday 24th. July 1827

Samuel Crawford)
        vs.   ) Appl.
Thomas Brandon) Applt.
                    The plaintiff in his proper person dismisses
his suit and the defendant assumes the payment of the cost.
Therefore it is considered that the plaintiff recover against
the Defendant and John Holmes Security for the prosecution
of his appeal his costs by him about his suit in this behalf
expended -

James Gibson   )
        vs.   )   Motion for judgment monies collected on
James McPherran)   Execution against Henry Dyche and not
                          paid over.
    The Plaintiff by his attorney moved the court for judg-
ment against the Defendant for monies collected on an
Execution and not paid over .
    Which motion was ordered to be entered for argument -

John Brown   ) Case
        vs.·   )
Samuel McKeehan) Contd. by consent

George Bell   )
        vs.   ) Certio
Henry A. Farnsworth)

The matters in dispute in this cause between the parties
are refered to the final determination of Thomas Temple, *
or a majority of them is to be made the judgment of the court
which is ordered accordingly - * Stephen Brooks and Christopher
(P-259) Tuesday 24th. July 1827. Kerby whose award thereupon

William Beard Pauper)
  vs.) Case
McKee L. Catter)
     By the Court Robert I. McKenney
is assigned as counsel to prosecute this suit on behalf of
the plaintiff -

George Alexander)
  vs.) Certio
Andrew Howell)
     On motion of Defendant by Attorney a
Rule is allowed him to shew cause why the Defendants petition
and writ should be dismissed -

John Baker)
  vs.) Certio
Howell Houston and)
William Houston) Continued as on affidavit plaintiff

State of Tennessee)
Howell Houston Prosr.) T. A. B.
  vs.)
John Gladin) Continued - John Gladin acknow-
       ledged to owe to the State of
Tennessee one hundred Dollars and Lewis Ball his surety also
acknowledged to owe the State of Tennessee fifty dollars
yet upon condition that if John Gladin shall make his personal appearance at the court of pleas and quarter sessions
to be held for the county of Greene in the Courthouse in
Greeneville on the Wednesday next after the fourth Monday in
October next and stand his trial in this prosecution against
him and not depart the court without leave the above (P-260)
recognizance to be void otherwise inforce Howell Houston the
prosecutor also acknowledged to owe the State of Tennessee
fifty dollars yet upon condition that if he shall make his
personal appearance at the court of pleas and quarter sessions to be held for the County of Greene in the Courthouse
in Greeneville on Wednesday next after the fourth Monday in
October next and prosecute and give evidence on behalf of
the State of Tennessee in this prosecution against John Gladin
and not depart the Court without leave then this recognizance
to be void otherwise in force -

John Balch)
  vs.) Certio
James McPherran)
     On motion ordered that the forfeiture
entered against William Barkley for failing to attend as a

witness in this suit at the last term of this court be set aside -

William Alexander   )
     vs.   ) Certio
John Light   )

        In this cause it is ordered that Alias Supersedeas be awarded to Greene County returnable here at next Court -

Simmons Crawford, Administrator)
of Jesse Winfrey, Decd.   ) Attachment
     vs.   )
Jonathan Wood   ) James Allen who has been
                         summoned as Garnishee in this cause appeared accordingly and being qualified according (P-261) to act of assembly deposes that at the time he was summoned as Garneshee he was not indebted to Jonathan Wood that he knows of no other person indebted to him, that he has none of the effects of the said Jonathan Wood in his hands except a tea canister with about six peace which the plaintiff releases and that he knows of no effects of the said Jonathan Wood in the hands of any other person -

    Therefore it is considered that the judgment - ni Si-entered against James Allen at the last term of this court as Garnishee be set aside, and that the said James Allen from the Garnishment aforesaid be discharged that the Scire Facias issued against James Allen as Garnishee be dismissed, and that the plaintiff pay the costs of this Garnishment -

    And Court adjourned untill tomorrow morning 10 o'clock

                                  Gilbert Woolsey
                                  A. Gillespie
                                  H. D. Hale
                                  Hugh Maloney

(P-262) Wednesday 25th. July 1827
     Court met present

    The Minutes of Yesterdays proceedings were read and signed -

State of Tennessee   )
Jacob Thornburg, Pros.) T. A. B.
     vs.   )
Elijah Nicholson   ) On motion and with the assent
                         of the Attorney General a Nolli Prosequi is entered in this prosecution the costs of which are assumed by the Defendant and thereupon Hugh D. Hale assumed for and on behalf of the Defendant the payment of the costs aforesaid and agrees that judgment be entered against him for the same. Therefore it is considered that the State of Tennessee recover against the said Hugh D. Hale the costs aforesaid according to his assumpsit -

George Bell)
    vs.) Certio
Henry A. Farnsworth)

        The refrees who were appointed to settle the matters in dispute between the parties in this cause this day made their award as follows -

    "Pursuant to order from the Worshipful Court of Greene County and to us directed (P-263) July Sess. 1827 we Thomas Temple, Stephen Brooks & Christopher Kirby after hearing the matters in dispute wherein George Bell is plaintiff and Henry A. Farnsworth Defendant are of opinion that Henry A. Farnsworth is indebted to sd. Bell the sum of seventeen dollars and thirty eight cents and one third cents and therefore sd. Farnsworth is to said Bell the aforesaid sum and also all costs according or said suit - Given under our hands on this 24th. July 1827 -

                Thos. Temple
                Stephen Brooks
                Christopher Kerby

    Upon consideration whereof it is considered that the award aforesaid be in all things affined and David Farnsworth Security for the prosecution of his writ of certiorari the aforesaid sum of seventeen dollars thirty eight and one third cents and his costs by him about his suit in this behalf expended -

Andrew Davis)
    vs.) On motion of Defendant by Attorney alias
Philip Harmon) writs of certiorari and supersedeas are
                awarded him returnable here at next court -

Joseph Davis & Moses G. Wilson)
    Guardians &c.) Petition &c.
    vs.)
Mary Keasling and Philip Harmon) Time to answer
Administrators of Jacob Keasling, Decd.) or plead untill
                                    next Court -

(P-264) Wednesday 25th. July 1827.
State of Tennessee)
    vs. Prosr.) On motion and with the assent of the
Elizabeth White) Attorney General a Nolli Prosequi is
) entered in this prosecution the costs
                  of which are assumed by John White for the Defendant. Therefore it is considered that the State of Tennessee recover against the said John White the costs aforesaid according to his assumpsit -

State of Tennessee
Kindness White, Prosr.

        On motion and with the assent of the Attorney General a Nolli Prosequi is entered in this prosecution the costs of which are assumed by John White for the Defendant. Therefore it is considered that the State of Tenn.

recover against the said John White the costs aforesaid
according to his assumpsit -

State of Tennessee   )
Benjamin Carter, Prosr.) Assault
    vs.   )
John Grymes   ) On motion and with the assent of
                      the Attorney General a Nolli
Prosequi is entered this prosecution the costs of which are
assumed by the (P-265) Defendant. Therefore it is considered
by the Court that the State of Tennessee recover against the
said John Grymes the costs of this suit according to his
assumpsit -

State of Tennessee   )
Andrew Stephens, Prosr.) On motion and with the assent of
Martin Cline   ) the Attorney General a Nolli
                    Prosequi is entered in this
prosecution the costs of which are assumed by the Defendant
in his proper person and thereupon Samuel Allen assumed for
and on behalf of the Defendant the payment of the costs aforesaid and agrees that judgment be entered against him for the
same -
    Therefore it is considered that the State of Tennessee
recover against the said Samuel Allen the costs aforesaid
according to his assumpsit -

State of Tennessee   )
Andrew Caldwell, Prosr.) Riot &c.
    vs.   )
Moses Shanks   ) This day came as well the Attorney
                    General as the Defendant in his
proper person and the Defendant in his proper person and
the Defendant being charged on the bill of Indictment for
plea thereto says that he is not guilty in manner and form
as charged in the Bill of Indictment and puts himself on the
Country and the Attorney General having done the like came
also a jury to wit Wyatt Hill, John Hunter, Edward Reed,
Jacob Bible, Thomas Lawson (P-266) Henry A. Farnsworth,
George Rightsell, Thomas Davis, Ephraim Wilson, Jacob Carter
Samuel McKeehen, Philip Harmon who being elected tried and
sworn the truth to speak upon this issue of Traverse upon
their oath do say that the Defendant is not guilty in manner
and form as charged in the Bill of Indictment -

    And on motion and for satisfactory reason appearing to
the Court - It is ordered that the costs of this prosecution
be paid by Andrew Caldwell the prosecutor -

State of Tennessee)
Turner Sharp, Prosr.) T. A. B.
    vs.   )
John Webb   ) This day came as well the Attorney
                General as the Defendant in his
proper person and the Defendant being charged on the Bill of

Indictment for plea thereto says that he is guilty in manner
and form as charged in the Bill of Indictment and puts himself on the Country and the Attorney General lying done the
same came also a jury to wit John Love, David Loagan, Frederick White, Samuel Allen, Henry Monteith, John White, Jacob
White, Aaron Mills, Jesse Reynolds, John Graymes, Jacob
Hoyal and Joseph Hunter who being elected tried and sworn
the truth to speak upon this issue of traverse upon their
oath do say that the Defendant is guilty in manner and form
as charged in the Bill of Indictment (P-267)   Therefore
it is considered that the Defendant for such his offence be
fined forfeit and pay to the State of Tennessee the sum of
twenty five cents and that he pay the costs of this prosecution -

State of Tennessee)
    vs.   ) Bastardy
George Rightsell)

    The Defendant who stands bound by recog-
nizance for his appearance here to answer the State of Tennessee for a charge alledged against him for begeting a Bastard
child of the body of Sarah Lucinda Stewart appeared accordingly and entered into bond in the sum of six hundred dollars
conditioned that he will perform such order as the court shall
from time to time make concerning the maintainance of said
child whereupon it is ordered that the Defendant pay the costs
in this behalf of the Defendant the payment of the fine and
costs aforesaid and agrees that judgment be entered against
him for the same -
    Therefore it is considered that the State of Tennessee
recover against the said Jacob Bible the fine and costs aforesaid according to his assumpsit -
(P-268) Wednesday 25th. July 1827 -

Sarah Lucinda Stewart)
    vs.   )   The plaintiff by his attorney
George M. Rightsell   )   James P. Taylor moved the court
    here for judgment against the
Defendant for the maintainance of a Bastard child begoten
of the body of the said Sarah Lucinda Stuart by the Defendant
for one year from the present court upon consideration whereof it is ordered by the Court that the plaintiff be allowed
the sum of forty dollars for the maintainance of said child
from one year from the present court and that said allowance
be paid by the Defendant and Jacob Bible his Security for the
maintainance of said child and also the costs of this motion -

    Of which judgment the plaintiff releases the sum of
$17.50 rec'd. in a cow and a note of hand -

State of Tennessee)
Ira Green, Prosr.)   Indictment for an Assault
    vs.   )
Jacob Hise   )   This day came as well the Attorney
    General as the Defendant in his
proper person and the Defendant being charged on the Bill of

Indictment for plea thereto says that he is guilty in manner
and form as therein against him is alledged and puts himself
on the Country and the Attorney General having done the same
came also a jury to wit John Craig, Nicholas Shanks, John
Mattsberger, Turner Sharp, John Crawford (P-269) Edward
Murphey, Henry Bowman, William Carter, William Cradrick,
Robert Erabson, John Reah, and John Casteel, who being elected
tried and sworn the truth to speak upon the issue of Traverse
upon their oath do say that the Defendant is guilty in manner
and form as charged in the Bill of Indictment. Therefore it
is considered that the Defendant for such his offence be
fined forfeit and pay to the State of Tennessee the sum of
one dollar, that he be counted to the common jail of Greene
County thereto remain untill three of the Clock on Tomorrow
that he pay the costs of this prosecution and is charged in
custody of the sheriff of Greene County untill Fine and costs
are paid - From which judgment the Defendant by Attorney prays
an appeal to the next circuit court of law to be held for the
County of Greene in the Courthouse in Greeneville on the first
Monday in September next and thereupon Jacob Hise acknowledged
to owe to the State of Tennessee one hundred dollars yet upon
condition that if Jacob Hise shall make his personal appearances at the Circuit Court of Law to be held for the County
of Greene in the Courthouse in Greeneville on Tuesday next
after the first Monday in September next and stand his trial
in this prosecution against him and not depart the court without leave then the above recognizance to be void otherwise
in force - And thereupon Ira Green acknowledged to owe the
State of Tennessee the sum of one hundred dollars yet upon
condition that if Ira Green shall make his personal appearance
at the Circuit Court (P-270) of Law to be held for the
County of Greene in the Courthouse in Greeneville on Tuesday
next after first Monday in September next and prosecute and
give evidence on behalf of the State of Tennessee against
Jacob Hise and not depart the Court without leave then the
above recognizance to be void otherwise in force. Whereupon
the Defendant appeal is allowed and the proceedings ordered
to be certified -

     And Court adjourned untill tomorrow morning 9 o'clock -

                                   A. Gillespie
                                   Cornelius Smith,J.P
                                   Joseph Brown, J.P.

     Thursday 26th. July 1827 -

     Court sat present

     The Minutes of Yesterdays proceedings were read and
signed -

State of Tennessee   )
     vs.   )   Sci Fa. Forftd. Recogn.
John Rimel   )
                       On motion and with the assent of the

149.

Court a Nolli Prosequi is entered in this prosecution the
Costs whereof are ordered to be paid by the Trustee of
Greene County -
(P-271) Thursday 26th. July 1827

State of Tennessee)
        vs.   ) Sci Fa. Foftd. Recog.
John Guin, Bail of)
John Rimel   ) On motion and with the assent of the
                      Court a Nolli Prosequi is entered in
this prosecution the costs of which are ordered to be paid
by the Trustee of Greene County -

State of Tennessee   )
        vs.   ) Sci Fa. Forftd. Recog.
Levi Dunn, Bail of Jno. Rimel)
                             On motion and with the
assent of the Court a Nolli Prosequi is entered in this
prosecution the costs whereof are order to be paid by the
Trustee of Greene County -

State of Tennessee)
        vs.   ) Sci Fa. Forftd. Recog.
Levi Dunn, Bail of)
John Rimel   ) On motion and with the assent of the
                      Court a Nolli Prosequi is entered in
this prosecution thecosts whereof are ordered to be paid by
the Trustee of Greene County -

State of Tennessee)
        vs.   ) Sci Fa. Foftd. Recog.
Levi Dunn, Bail of)
John Rimel   ) On motion and with the assent of the
                      Court a Nolli Prosequi is entered in
this prosecution the costs whereof an ordered to be paid by
the Trustee of Greene County.
(P-272) Thursday 26th. July 1827.

State of Tennessee)
        vs.   ) Sci Fa. Forftd. Recog.
John Guin, Bail of)
John Rimel   ) On motion and with the assent of the
                      Court a Nolli prosequi is entered in
this prosecution the costs of which are ordered to be paid
by the Trustee of Greene County -

Benedict Hoyal   )
     vs.   ) Case
Daniel Linebough)
                     Ordered by the Court that this cause be
struck from the Docket and that the plaintiff pay the costs
of the same -

Abraham Peters   )
     vs.   ) Covt.
Daniel Borden and John M. Kilgore)

Ordered by the Court that this cause be struck from
the Docket and that the costs of the same be paid by the
plaintiff -

Jacob M. Bewley   )
    vs.   )   Case
William Herring   )

          Ordered by the Court that this cause
be struck from the Docket and that the Costs of the same be
paid by the plaintiff -
(P-273) Thursday 26th. July 1827

Joseph Davis and Moses G. Wilson)
    Guardians &c.   )   Petition &c.
      vs.   )
Philip Harmon & Mary Keasling   )   On motion the order given
Admrs. of Jacob Keasling Decd.   )   Defendants time to answer
                or plead untill next Court
is set aside -

State of Tennessee   )
Howell Houston, Prosr.   )   T. A. B. on Thomas Batt
    vs.   )
Samuel Allen   )   On motion and with the assent of the
          Court a Nolli Prosequi is entered
          in this prosecution - the costs
of which are ordered to be paid by the Trustee of Greene
County except the Attorney General taxed fee which he now
releases -

State of Tennessee   )
Philip Cummings, Prosr.)   T. A. B.
    vs.   )
John Muncher   )   Continued on affida vit of Defend-
          ant, John Muncher acknowledged to
owe the State of Tennessee one hundred dollars and James W,
Wyly his Surety also acknowledged to owe the Sta te of Tennessee fifty dollars yet upon condition that if John Muncher
shall make his personal appearance at the Court of Plea s and
quarter Sessions to be held for the County of Greene in the
Courthouse in Greeneville on Wednesday next after the fourth
Monday in October next stand his trial in this prosecution
against (P-274) him and not depart the Court without leave
then above recognizance to be void otherwise in force -

State of Tennessee)
John Muncher, prosr.)   T. A. B.
    vs.   )
Philip Cummins   )   Continued on affidavit of Defendant
          Philip Cummins acknowledged to owe
the State of Tennessee one hundred dollars and James Jennings
his surety also acknowledged to owe the State of Tennessee
fifty dollars yet upon condition that if Philip Cummings shall
make his personal appearance at the Court of Pleas and quarter
sessions to be held for the County of Greene in the Courthouse
in Greeneville on Wednesday next after the fourth Monday in

October next and stand his trial in this prosecution against him and not depart the Court without leave then the above recognizance to be void otherwise in force -

Daniel M. Guin   )
          vs.   )   Appeal
Ephraim Wilson, Applt.)

          This day came the parties by attor-
nies and thereupon a jury to wit John Hunter, Wyatt Hill,
William Craddick, Robert Brabson, Aaron Mills, Jesse Reynolds
John Casteel, David Key, Andrew Roberts, Samuel McKeehan,
Jacob Carter, and Thomas Lawson who being elected tried and
sworn well and truly to try the matters in dispute between
the parties upon their oath do say that (P-275) they find
for the plaintiff Twenty five dollars - Therefore it is considered that the plaintiff recover against the Defendant and
James Wright Security for the prosecution of the Defendants
appeal the aforesaid sum of Twenty five dollars and his costs
by him about his suit in this behalf expended -

James Gillespie)
          vs.   )   Case in Assumpsit
Allen Gillespie)
                       Continued as on affidavit plaintiff -

James McPherson)
          vs.   )   Certio
James Gibson   )

          This day came the parties by attornies
and thereupon a jury to wit, John Love, James Park, Samuel
Allen, Daniel Allen, Martin Cline, Henry Fearle, Levi Dunn,
Clement Reynolds, John Glass, Thomas Davis, Joseph Hunter
and William Ross (of John) who being elected tried and
sworn well and truly to try this cause upon their oath do
say that they find for the Defendant. Therefore it is considered that the plaintiff take nothing by his suit and that
the Defendant recovers against the plaintiff his costs by
him about his suit in this behalf expended -

Daniel Allen executor   )
of Hannah Baker .Decd.   )   Certio
          vs.   )
Isaac Baker   )   Continued on affidavit   Howell
                               Houston.

(P-276) Thursday 26th. July 1827.
Daniel Casteel)
          vs.   )   Certio
Omy Malone   )

          This day came the parties by attornies
and thereupon a jury to wit John Love, James Park, Samuel
Allen, Daniel Allen, Martin Cline, Henry Feasle, Levi Dunn,
Clement Reynolds, John Glass, Thomas Davis, Joseph Hunter
and William Ross (of John) who being elected tried and sworn
well and truly to try this cause.

The plaintiff by Attorney suffers a Non Suit.

Therefore it is considered that the plaintiff take nothing by his suit and that the Defendant recover against the plaintiff her costs by her about her suit in this behalf expended -

Daniel Casteel)
    vs.) Certio
John Casteel)

    This day came the parties by attornies and thereupon a jury to wit, John Love, James Park, Samuel Allen, Daniel Allen, Martin Cline, Henry Feasle, Levi Dunn, Clement Reynolds, John Glass, Thomas Davis, Joseph Hunter, and William Ross (of John) who being elected tried and sworn well and truly to try this cause.

    The plaintiff by attorney suffers a non suit.

    Therefore it is considered that the plaintiff take nothing by his suit and that the Defendant recover against the plaintiff his costs by him about his suit in this behalf expended.

(P-277) Thursday 26th. July 1827.

John Long)
    vs.) Appeal
John Dickson, Applt.)

    On motion and for reasons disclosed by affidavit Robert I. McKenney Attorney for plaintiff this cause is continued untill the next court.

    Grand and Pettit Jurors discharged 3 days.

William Dickson)
    vs.) Sci Fa. For Debt and Costs
Thomas Battersley)

    This day came the parties by attornies and the Defendant by attorney with drawing the plea of payment confesses that he owe the plaintiff the sum of one hundred and four dollars and forty cents with the interest thereon from the 4th. day of February 1824. Therefore it is considered that the plaintiff may have execution against the defendant for the sum of one hundred and four dollars and forty cents the debt in the Scire Facias named with the further sum of fifteen dollars and fifty one cents for interest due and accrued thereon - and that the plaintiff recover against the Defendant the sum of eighty dollars and thirty four cents for original costs by him about his suit in this behalf expended and also his cost expended in sueing forth and prosecuting his writ of Scire Facias

    And Court adjourned untill tomorrow morning 9 o'clock

                    Joseph Brown, J.P.
                    Cornelius Smith, J.P
                    John Balch, J. P.

(P-278) Friday 27th. July 1827.

    Court met present

    The Minutes of yesterdays proceedings were read and signed -

Robert H. Wilson)
    vs.   ) Case
George Smith   )

Time to plead so as not to delay

William Stanley)
    vs.   ) Trespass
Charles Gass   )

Time to plead so as not to delay

Joseph Hays)
    vs.   ) Covenant
John Davis   )

Demurrer to Declaration

This day came the parties by attornies and thereupon the Defendants Demurrer to the plaintiffs Declaration came on for argument whereupon all and singular the premises being seen and by the court fully understood. It is considered that the Demurrer aforesaid be accrued and that the plaintiff recover against the Defendant his Damages by occasion in the Declaration mentioned but because it is unknown to the court what those Damages are It is   (P-279) ordered that a jury come here at the next Term of this court to enquire of Damages between the parties in this suit -

William Brown   )
    vs.   ) Motion to correct &c.
Isaac Jones & Mitchell Bright)

Cont'd by consent.

George Rinker)
    vs.   ) Covt.
John Balch   )

Time to plead so as not to delay.

George Alexander)
    vs.   ) Certio
Andrew Howell)

Rule to Quash

This day came the parties by attornies and the Defendant by Attorney discharges the Rule heretofore entered to quash the proceedings before the justice of the peace -

And on motion of plaintiff by attorney a rule is allowed him to shew cause why the Defendants petition and writ of certiorari should be dismissed -

Whereupon argument of counsel being heard all and singular the premises being seen and by the court fully understood It is considered that said Rule be discharged -

William Beard (Pauper))
    vs.   ) Case
McKee and Cutler   )

This writ issued in this cause being returned executed on Joseph (P-280) Cutler and that William McKee is not found. Therefore on motion a judicial attachment against the estate of William McKee is awarded him returnable here at next court

Mordecai Lincoln, Chairman)
of the Court of Pleas &c.) Debt
 VS.)
Joseph Brown, William K. Vance) Demurrer to Declaration
John Gass, & John Malony Senr.)

 This day came the parties by attornies and thereupon that the Defendants Demurrer to the plaintiff Declaration came on for argument whereupon all and singular the premises being seen and by the Court fully understood. It is considered that said Demurrer be overruled and that the said Defendants may have time to plead so as not todelay -

Hugh Murray)
 vs.) Certio
Abner Williams)

 This day came the plaintiff by Attorney and the Defendant although solemnly called came not but made default. Therefore it is considered that the plaintiff recover against the Defendant the sum of fifty five dollars with interest - thereon from the fourteenth day of December one thousand (P-281) eight hundred and twenty three and his costs by him about his suit in this behalf expended -

William Dickson)
 vs.) Attachment
John Cannon)

 This day came the plaintiff by attorney and the Defendant although solemnly called came not but made Default. Therefore it is considered that the plaintiff recover against the Defendant the sum of ninety nine dollars and fifty Seven cents the Residue of the Debt in the Declaration mentioned and his costs by him about his suit in this behalf expended -

William Ripley)
 vs.) The petition of the defendant was presented
James Hise) by Aaron Finch his Attorney praying writs
 of Certiorari and Supersedeas upon consideration whereuf it is ordered that writs issue pursuant to the prayer of said petition returnable here at next Court -

James Gibson)
 vs.) Motion &c.
James McPherran)

 This day came the parties by Attornies and thereupon the motion entered against the Defendant at the present term of this court fully understood It is considered by the court came on for argument whereupon all and singular the premises being seen and by the court fully understood

It is considered by the Court that the plaintiff (P-282) recover against the Defendant the sum of ninety dollars and eighty six six cents being the amount of the principal collected by the said Defendant with interest thereon for sixteen years and his costs by him about his suit in this behalf expended -

Judgment 8th. December 1810 $ 46.36
    Interest 16 Years   44.50
                                      $ 90.86

And Court adjourned untill court in course untill which time all matters and things in the same depending and undetermined are continued -

                                    Henry Dyche
                                    Christian Dyche
                                    John Balch

(P-283)   State of Tennessee
      At a Court of Pleas and Quarter Sessions continued and held for the County of Greene in the Courthouse in Greeneville on the fourth Monday being the 22nd. day of October one thousand eight hundred and twenty seven   was present

Moses G. Wilson and   )
Joseph Davis Guardians &c.)   The petitioners in their proper
       vs.   )   persons appeared in court and
Mary Keasling and Philip   )   dismissed their petition and
Harmon Admr. &c.   )   the Defendants assume the payment
                              of the costs. Therefore it is considered that the petitioners recover against the Defendants their costs in this behalf expended -

Nicholas Shanks   )
    vs.   )   Ca. Sa. Issued by a Justice of the
Jacob Hoyal   )   Peace & Bond returned for appearance &c.

               On motion of Defendant by Attorney a Rule is allowed him to shew cause why the proceedings in this cause should be quashed -
(P-284)   Monday 22nd. Octr. 1827 -

State of Tennessee   )
    vs.   )   Bastardy
Isaac Fox   )
                The Defendant who stands bound by Recognizance for his appearance to answer the State of Tennessee of a charge alledged against him for begeting a Bastard Child of the body of Milam Reeves of this Country single woman appeared accordingly and entered into bond in the sum of six hundred dollars with James Hise and Daniel Guin Securities conditioned for the maintainance of said child whereupon it is ordered that the said Isaac Fox pay the costs in this behalf expended -

State of Tennessee)
      vs.   ) Bastardy
Frederick Fraker   )

        The Defendant who stands bound by recognizance for his appearance here to answer the State of Tennessee of a charge alledged against him for begeting a Bastard Child of the body Ann Harrison of this county single woman appeared accordingly and entered into bond in sum of six hundred dollar with Adam Fraker security continued for the maintainance of said child whereupon it is ordered that the said Frederick Fraker pay the costs in this behalf expended -

David Keller   )
      vs.   )   Certio
Benjamin Keller)

        The petition of the Defendant (P-235) was presented by James W. Wyly his attorney praying writs of certiorari and supersedeus upon consideration whereof it is ordered that writs issue pursuant to the prayer of said petition on Bond and Security being given as the law directs
        And Court adjourned untill tomorrow morning 9o'clock
                        Thomas Jones, J.P.
                        Joseph Brown, J.P.
                        Jess Kerby,   J.P.
                        A. Gillespie

Tuesday 23rd. October 1827.

Court met present

        The Minutes of yesterdays proceedings were read and signed.

John Balch   )
      vs.   ) Certio
James McPherran)

        Continued as on affidavit of plaintiff

The Heirs of John Russell Decd.)
      vs.   ) Covent.
Samuel Bridewell   )

        Continued by consent.

(P-236)   Tuesday 23rd. Octr. 1827.

James Gillespie)
      vs.   ) Case in Assumpsit
Allen Gillespie   )

        Continued as in affidavit plaintiff commissions are awarded the plaintiff to take the depositions of Nathaniel Hays of Monroe County and William E. Gillespie of Maury County by giving the Defendant twenty days notice of the time and place of executing such commissions - A commission is also awarded the Defendant to take the deposition of Isaac Wilson of Washington County by giving the plaintiff five days notice of the time and place of executing such commission all of which may be directed to any one justice of the peace for either of the aforesaid counties - -

John Baker   )
    vs.   )   Certio
Howell Houston and)
William Houston   )   Continued on affidavit of William
                            Houston - A commission is awarded
the Defendants to take the Deposition of Isaac Baker James
Baker and Absalom Houston of Monroe County which may be
directed to any one Justice of the Peace for said County
by giving the plaintiff ten days notice of the time and
place of executing such commission -
(P-287)   Tuesday 23rd. Octr. 1827

        Richard M. Woods, esquire high sheriff in and for the
County of Greene returns here into open court the State
writ of Venire Facias to him directed endorsed "Returnable
Tuesday after the fourth Monday in October - Issd. 13th.
Augt. 1827" executed on all but John K. Gammon "R.M. Woods,
Shff.

        Out of whom are selected as the Statutes in that case
provides the following gentlemen as Grand Inquest and Jury
to wit - Casper Easterly appointed forman by the court.
James Morrow, Jacob T. Wyrick, David Frazier, James Biggs,
John Johnson. David Rankin, John Dunwoody, Thomas H. Wilson,
John Britton, Joseph Reader, Daniel Smith, John Dodd Junr.
        Good and lawful men of the County of Greene aforesaid
who being now here empannelled and sworn in the Courthouse
in Greeneville to enquire for the State aforesaid and for the
body of the County of Greene aforesaid received their charge
and retired from the Bar.   (3 Days Each)

        Lofton Sherill, a constable was qualified to attend the
above Grand Jury in 3 days Certf. issd.

        Samuel Jones to attend on the Court. 3 days cert. issd.

        Thomas Mitchell summoned to attend the present court
as a Juror for Satisfactory reasons appearing to the Court
is released from further attendance as such -
(P-288) Tuesday 23rd. Octr. 1827

        The following persons being the Residue of the Venire
to the present court are to attend the same as Pettit jurors
respectively untill discharged to wit William Snyder,
Joseph Johnson, John Neese, Thomas Cremer, John Houston,
Daniel Delany, Asaiah Haynes, Jacob Krauss.

George Squib   )
for John A. McKenney   )   Order Sale
    vs.   )
Moses Vanscoysc   )   James Britton a constable of Greene
                            County returned here into court an
execution issued by Joseph Brown esquire an acting Justice
of the Peace for said County against the estate of the Defendant for the sum of fifty six dollars and sixty cents debt and

the further sum of Two Dollars Twenty five cents cost recovered by the plaintiff against the Defendant before said justice on the 22nd. day of September 1827. On Which execution said constable has made return "Search made and no personal property of the Deft found in my County of which to make the money I therefore levied this execution on all the right, title, interest and claim that Moses Vanscoysc has of in and to about 67 acres of land on the Waters of little Chuckey joining lands of John Hall & Mrs. Smelsor this this 27th. September 1827. Jas. Britton, Constable" Therefore on motion of the plaintiff by Robert I. McKenney his Attorney It is considered that all the right, title, interest, claim and demand of the said Moses Vanscoysc of in and to the aforesaid tract of land be condemned to the satisfaction of (P-289) the Recovery and that the same or so much thereof as will satisfy said recovery and the costs of this motion be sold as the law directs.

Daniel Allen, executor)
of Hannah Baker Decd.)   Certio
    vs.   )
Isaac Baker   )   This day came the parties by
                              Attornies and thereupon a jury
to wit John Neese, William Snyder, Joseph Johnson, James McCord, Samuel McKeehan, Jacob Newman, Robert Craig, John T. Vestal, Nicholas Shanks, Samuel Mitchell, John Kennedy and Charles Isacs who being elected tried and sworn well and truly to try this cause upon their oath do say that they find for the plaintiff eleven dollars and thirty five cents. Therefore it is considered that the plaintiff recover against the Defendant and John Gladin Securoty for the prosecution of the plaintiffs writ of certiorari the aforesaid sum of eleven dollars and thirty five cents and his costs by him about his suit in this behalf expended -

From which judgment the Defendant by Attorney prays an appeal to the next Circuit Court of Greene County to be held for the County of Greene in the Court house in Greeneville on the first Monday in March next and having given bond and security to prosecute his appeal is granted and the proceedings ordered to be certified -

State of Tennessee   )
Howell Houston, Prosr.)   T. A. B.
    vs.   )
John Gladin   )   This day came as well the Attorney
                             (P-290) General as the Defendant
in his proper person and the Defendant being charged on the Bill of Indictment for plea thereto says that he is guilty in manner and form as therein against him is alledged and puts himself on the mercy of the Court. Therefore it is considered that the Defendant for such his offence be fined forfeit. and pay to the State of Tennessee one dollar and that he pay the costs of this prosecution -

State of Tennessee)
Nancy Cummings, Prosr.)   T. A. B.
      vs.)
John Muncher)   On motion and with the assent
                           of the Court a Nolli Prosequi
is entered in this prosecution and the costs of the same
assumed by the Defendant - And thereupon Philip Cummings
assumed for and on behalf of the Defendant for the payment
of the costs aforesaid and agrees that judgment be entered
against him for the same - Therefore it is considered that
the State of Tennessee recover against the said Philip
Cummings the cost aforesaid according to his assumpsit -

State of Tennessee)
Mary Cumming, Prosr.)   T. A. B.
      vs.)
John Muncher)   On motion and with the assent of the
                           court a Nolli Prosequi is entered in
this prosecution and the costs of the same assumed by Defendant and thereupon Philip Cummings assumed for and on behalf
of the Defendant the payment of the costs aforesaid and agrees
that judgment be entered against him for the same - Therefore
it is considered that the State of Tennessee recover against
the said Philip Cummings the costs aforesaid according to
his assumpsit -

State of Tennessee)
John Muncher, Prosr.)   T. A. B.
      vs.)
Philip Cummings)   On motion and with the assent of
                           the court a Nolli Prosequi is enter-
ed in this prosecution and the costs of the same are assumed
by the Defendant - and   (P-291)   thereupon John Muncher
in his proper person appeared in court and assumed for and
on behalf of the Defendant the payment of the costs aforesaid
and agree that judgment be entered against him for the same -
Therefore it is considered that the State of Tennessee recover
against the said John Muncher the costs aforesaid according
to his assumpsit -

John Brown)
      vs.)   Case
Samuel McKeehan)
               This day came the parties by attornies
and thereupon   a jury to wit, Thomas Cremer, John Houston,
Daniel Delany, Asariah Haynes, Abraham Dearstone, James Goodin,
West Haworth, Joseph Malone, William Stanley, Thomas Pogue
Evan Guin, and John Hoyal who being elected tried and sworn
the truth to speak upon the Issue joined upon their oath do
say that the Defendant is guilty in manner and form as the
plaintiff against him in his declaration hath complained and
they do assess the plaintiffs Damages by occasion thereof to
twenty five dollars. Therefore it is considered that the
plaintiff recover against the Defendant the Damages by the
jury aforesaid assessed and his cost by him about his suit in
this behalf expended -
(P-292) Tuesday 23rd. Octr. 1827.

William Smith, assignee)
John M. Kilgore) Covenant
vs.)
John Stephens) This day came the parties by
                     Attornies and thereupon a jury
to wit Jacob Krouss, James Kelly, Jonathan Ellis, James
Campbell, John Robinson, Martin Bailey, William Cradick,
Charles Nicholas, Abner Babb, John Shields, Michael Basinger
and Thomas McCord, who being elected tried and sworn well
and truly to this cause upon their oath do say that the defendant hath not kept and preformed his covenant as in pleading he hath alledged but hath broken the same in manner and
form as the plaintiff against him in his declaration hath
complained and they do assess the plaintiffs damages by
occasion thereof to two hundred and thirty eight dollars.
     Therefore it is considered that the plaintiff recover
against the Defendant the Damages by the jury aforesaid
assessed and his cost by him about his suit in this behalf
expended -

Joseph Hays)
vs.) Covt. Writ of Enquiry
John Davis)
     This day came the plaintiff by attorney and
thereupon a jury to wit Jacob Krouss, James Kelly, Jonathan
Ellis, James Campbell, John Robinson, Martin Bailey, William
Cradick, Charles Nicholas, Abner Babb, John Shields, Michael
Baysinger, and Thomas McCord who being elected tried and
sworn well, (P-295) and truly to enquire of Damages between
the parties upon their oath do say that the plaintiff hath
sustained damages by occasion in the Declaration mentioned
to one hundred and seventy seven dollars and fifty cents -
Therefore it is considered by the court that the plaintiff
recover against the Defendant the Damages by the jury aforesaid assessed and his cost by him about his suit in this
behalf expended -

William M. P. Mitchell)
vs.) Certio
John Graham)

                     Continued as on affidavit of
                     Defendant -

Mordecia Lincoln, Chairman)
of Court of Pleas &c.) Debt
vs.)
Joseph Brown, John Gass,) Continued as on affidavit
William K. Vance and) of Defendant -
John Malony heirs.)

John Long)
vs.) Appl. from Justice
John Dickson, Applt.)
                     This day came the parties by
Attornies and thereupon a jury to wit Jacob Krouss, James
Kelly, Jonathan Ellis, James Campbell, John Robinson, Martin

Bailey, William Cradick, Charles Nicholas, Abner Babb, John
Shields, Michael Baysinger and Thomas McCord who being
elected tried and sworn well and truly to try this cause
upon their (P-294) oath do say that they find for the
plaintiff Twenty Dollars.

And on motion of Defendant by Attorney a Rule is
allowed him to shew why a new trial should be granted - and
on argument It is ordered that said rule be made absolute -

George Davis)
vs.) Certio
Moses G. Wilson)

The petition of the Defendant was presented
by James W. Wyly his attorney praying writs of certiorari
and supersedeas - Upon consideration whereof it is ordered
that writs issue pursuant to the prayer of said petition on
bond and security being given according to law -

John Gass, Senr.)
vs.) Certio
Elijah Parkins and)
Joseph Moore) The petition of the Defendants was
presented by Robert J. McKenney their
attorney praying writs of certiorari and superdeas upon
consideration whereof it is ordered that writs issue pursuant
whereof it is ordered that writs issue pursuant to the prayer
of said petition on bond and security being given according
to (P-295) And Court adjourned untill tomorrow morning 10
o'clock.

> Joseph Brown, J.P.
> Cornelius Smith, J.P.
> Henry Dyche, J.P.

Wednesday 24th. Octr. 1827.

Court met present

The Minutes of Yesterdays proceedings were read and
signed -

William Alexander)
vs.) Certio
John Light)
On motion of plaintiff by Attorney a
Rule is allowed him to shew cause why
the Defendants petition and writs of certiorari should be
dismissed -

Ordered by the Court that the same rule entered in the
Circuit court respecting the Continances of causes be
adopted as a Rule in this Court -
(P-296) Wednesday 24th. Octr. 1827

John Brown)
vs.) T. V. A.
Samuel McKeehan)

From the judgment ordered in this cause at the present
Term of this court the defendant by Attorney prays an appeal
to the next Circuit Court of Law to be held for the County
of Greene in the Courthouse in Greeneville on the first
Monday in March next and having given bond and security to
prosecute has appeal is granted and the proceedings ordered
to be certified -

State of Tennessee)
and James Davis)   Surety of the Peace Required
    vs.)
James Barnes)   James Barnes appeared in court and
                     acknowledged to owe the State of
Tennessee five hundred dollars and William Brothertin Senr.
his surety also acknowledged to owe the State of Tennessee
Two hundred and fifty dollars. Yet upon condition that if
James Barnes shall keep the peace towards all good people of
the State of Tennessee for the space of one year and one day
from the present time but specially towards James Davis --
    Whereupon it is considered that the Defendant pay the
costs in this behalf expended - And thereupon William Brothertin in his proper person assumed for and on behalf of the
Defendant the payment of the cost aforesaid - Therefore it
is considered that the State of Tennessee recover against
the said William Brothertin the costs aforesaid according
to his assumpsit -
(P-297)   Wednesday 24th. Octr. 1827.

    The Court being in session and siting as commitning
Magistrates ordered that James Barnes enter into Recognizance
himself into the sum of five hundred dollars for his appearance at the regular term of the circuit court to answer a
charge for an assault and battery on James Davis with and
intent to kill and murder
    And thereupon James Barnes acknowledged to owe the State
of Tennessee the sum of one thousand dollars and William
Brothertin Senr. his surety acknowledged to owe the State
of Tennessee five hundred dollars yet upon condition that
if James Barnes shall make his personal appearance at the
Circuit Court of Law to be held for the County of Greene in
the Court house in Greeneville on Wednesday next after the
first Monday in March next and answer the State of Tennessee
on the foregoing charge and not depart the Court without
leave then the above recognizance to be void otherwise in
force -

    Ordered that Martin Bailey for a contempt offered to
the Court in Session be fined the sum of Two Dollars and
fifty cents and that execution issue for the Same -
(P-298)

William Stanley)
    vs.)   Trespass
Charles Gass)
                   This day came the parties by Attornies

and thereupon a jury to wit Jacob Kross, Daniel Guin, John Moese, Joseph Johnson, Samuel K. Gauntt, William Alexander (of Geo.) James Campbell, John Fraker Junr. William Snyder Thomas Pogue, William Carter, and William Brown who being elected tried and sworn well and truly to try this cause –

By consent were respeted from rendering their verdict untill tomorrow –

State of Tennessee   )
Joseph Hunter Prosr.   )   T. A. B. on Prosr.
   vs.   )
Martin Bailey   )   This day came as well the Attorney
                                  General as the Defendant in his
proper person and the Defendant being charged on the Bill of Indictment for plea thereto says that he is not guilty in manner and form as therein against him is alledged and puts himself on the Country and the Attorney General having done the same came also a jury to wit Thomas Cremer, John Houston, Daniel Delany, Ozariah Haynes, John Weston, William Stanley James Goodin, John T. Vestal, James Anderson, Charles Nicholas, John Pogue, and Joseph Broner who being elected tried and sworn the truth to speak upon this issue of traverse were respected from rendering their verdict by consent untill tomorrow (P-299) Wednesday 24th. Octr. 1827

State of Tennessee   )
  John Milburn prosr.   )   Indict for Adultery
   vs.   )
Catharine Rhea   )   This day came as well the Attorney
                                  General as the Defendant in her
proper person and the Defendant being charged on the Bill of Indictment for plea thereto says that she is guilty in manner and form as charged in the Bill of Indictment and puts herself on the mercy of the court – Therefore it is considered by the Court that the Defendant for such her offence be fined forfeit and pay to the State of Tennessee the sum of twenty five cents and that she pay the costs of this prosecution –and thereupon Joseph McCurry in his proper person assumed for and on behalf of the Defendant the payment of the fine and costs aforesaid and agrees that judgment be entered against him for the same – Therefor it is considered that the State of Tennessee recover against the said Joseph McCurry the fine and costs aforesaid according to his assumpsit –

State of Tennessee   )
John Millburn Prosr.)   Indict. for Adultery
   vs.   )
Joseph McCurry   )   This day came as well the Attorney
                             General as the Defendant in his
proper person and the Defendant being charged on the Bill of Indictment for plea thereto says that he is not guilty in manner and form as therein against him is alledged and puts (P-300) himself on the Country and the Attorney General done the same, came also a jury to wit Seburn Jewell, James Lackland, Andrew Howell, William Luster, William Brannon,

Charles Goss, James Guin, James McKahan, William Cradick, John Crabtree, Alexander Laughlin and John Reah, who being elected tried and sworn the truth to speak upon this issue of traverse upon their oath do say that the Defendants is Guilty in manner and form as charged in the Bill of Indictment. Therefore it is considered by the Court that the Defendant for such his offence be fined forfeit and pay to the State of Tennessee the sum of Twenty Dollars that he be comited to the common jail of Greene County thereto remain until 12 of the clock tomorrow & that he pay the costs of this prosecution -

State of Tennessee)
Reah, Prosr.) T. A. B.
  vs.)
John Millburn) Continued as on affidavit of Defendant, John Millburn acknowledged to owe the State of Tennessee five hundred dollars yet upon condition that if John Millburn shall make his personal appearance at the Court of Pleas and Quarter Sessions to be held for the County of Greene in the Courthouse in Greeneville on Wednesday next after the fourth Monday in January next and stand his trial in this prosecution against him and not depart the court without leave then this recognizance to be void otherwise in force -
(P-301) Wednesday 24th. Octr. 1827.

State of Tennessee)
  vs.) Bastardy
Abraham B. Boin)

    The Defendant who stands found by recognizance for his appearance here to answer the State of Tennessee of a charge alledged against him for begeting a Bastard child of the body of Jane Robinson of this County single woman appeared accordingly and entered into Bond in the sum of six hundred dollars with Joseph Davis security continued for the maintainance of said child - Whereupon it is considered that the Defendant pay the fine and also the costs in this behalf expended - And thereupon Joseph Davis assumed for and on behalf of the Defendant the payment of the fine and costs aforesaid - Therefore it is considered that the State of Tennessee recover against the said Joseph Davis the fine and costs aforesaid according to his assumpsit -

State of Tennessee)
  vs.) Bastardy
Melinda Fielder)

    The Defendant who stand bound by recognizance for the appearance to answer the State of Tennessee of a charge alledged against her of having been delivered of a Bastard child of which she refuses to declare the father appeared accordingly and entered into bond in the sum of six hundred dollars with Elizabeth Corder Security continued for the maintainance of said child - Whereupon it is ordered that the Defendant pay the costs in this behalf expended - and

(P-302) thereupon Elijah Corder assumed for and on behalf of the Defendant the payment of the costs aforesaid and agrees that judgment be entered against him for the same - Therefore it is considered the State of Tennessee recover against the said Elijah Corder the costs aforesaid according to his assumpsit -

And Court adjourned untill tomorrow morning 9 o'clock

Joseph Brown, J.P.
A . Gillespie, J.P.
Cornelius Smith, J.P.

Thursday 25th. Octr. 1827

Court met present

The Minutes of yesterdays proceedings were read and signed -

William Stanley)
vs.) Trespass
Charles Gass)

This day came the parties by attornies and thereupon the jury who were respeted from rendering their verdict on yesterday to wit Daniel Guin, Jacob Kross, John Neese, Joseph Johnson, Samuel K. Gauntt, William Alexander (of Geo.) James Campbell, John Fraker Junr. William Snyder, Thomas Pogue, William Carter and William Brown who returned to the Bar and declared they could not agree, whereupon by consent a juror (P-303) is withdrawn and a mistrial entered-

State of Tennessee)
Joseph Hunter, Prosr.) T.A.B.
vs.)
Martin Bailey)

This day came as well the Attorney General as the Defendant in his proper person and thereupon the jury who were respeted from rendering their verdict on yesterday to wit Thomas Cremer, John Houston, Daniel Delany, Asariah Haynes, John Weston, William Hanley, James Goodin, John T. Vestal, James Anderson, Charles Nicholas, John Pogue and Joseph Bruner -

Who returned to the Bar and declared they could not agree whereupon by consent a juror is withdrawn and a mistrial entered -

And thereupon Martin Bailey acknowledged to owe the State of Tennessee one hundred dollars yet upon condition that if he the said Martin Bailey shall make his personal appearance at the court of pleas and quarter sessions to be held for the County of Greene in the Courthouse in Greeneville on Wednesay next after the fourth Monday in January next and stand his trial in this prosecution against him and not depart the court without leave then the above recognizance to be void otherwise in force -

William Dickson)
  vs.   ) Attachment
Jonas Trobough)

      Rule to declare untill next court.

(P-304) Thursday 25th. Octr. 1827

William Dickson
for Alexander William's use Plff.   )Sci Fa. in Debt
  vs.   )
Charles Neilson, Archibald D. Neilson) Judgment $66715
Sarah L. Neilson, James R. Garrett and Jane) Costs   7.12½
his wife formerly Jane Neilson   ) The Scire Facias
Joseph S. Chunn and Catherine his wife) in this cause
formerly Catharine Neilson, Philip   ) being returned
H. Neilson, Robert Strong, Charles   ) on all but Rob-
Reedy and Martha his wife formerly) ert Strong and
Martha Strong, Green K. Cessna   ) two Sci Fa issued
and George Gillespie and Anna   ) against him and
formerly Anna Neilson his wife heirs) returned not found
at Law -   )
of Robert Neilson Decd.   )
      Defendants.   )

                This day came the
plaintiff by Attorney and the Defendants not appearing nor do
they say anything in bar of the Sci Facias the plaintiff
aforesaid whereby the plaintiff remains against the said
defendants therein undefended -
   Therefore it is considered by the court that the plaintiff
may have execution of the Debt and costs in the writ of Scire
Facias aforesaid named of the real estate of the said Robert
Neilson decd. which descended to the Defendants, together
with interest from the twenty seventh day of April one thous-
and eight hundred and twenty seven until paid and that the
plaintiff recover against the Defendants his costs by him
expended in sueing forth and prosecuting his writ of Scire
Facias -(P-305)
   Thursday 25th. October 1827

McKee & Cutler)
  vs.   ) Attachment
Hentle W. Atkinson)

      This day came the plaintiff by attorney
and the Defendant although solemnly ca led came not but made
default- Therefore it is considered that the plaintiff recover
against the Defendant their Damages by occasion in the Declaration mentioned - But because it is unknown to the Court what
those Damages are -
   It is ordered that a jury came here at the next Term of
this Court to enquire of Dama ges between the parties in this
Suit -

Marmaduke Lamb)
  vs.   ) Case
Samuel Walker)

      On motion of plaintiff by attorney ordered
by the court that the Defendants seventh plea be stricken out-

To which opinion and ordered the Defendants by Attorney tenders a Bill of exceptions which is signed and sealed and ordered to be made a part of the Record of this suit -

George Rinker Assignee)
  Simeon Parkin)   Covenant
     vs.)
John Balch)   This day came the parties by
                   attornies and thereupon a jury
to wit Richard West, Joseph Hunter, John Hoy, Edward L. Russell, Robert H. Wilson, Cornelius Hughes, Daniel Olinger, (P-306) James McKeehan, William Cradick, Seburn Jewell, Jacob Hoyal, and Martin Bailey who being elected tried and sworn the truth to speak upon the issue joined upon their oath do say that the Defendant hath not kept and performed his covenant as in pleading he hath alledged but hath broken the same in manner and form as the plaintiff against him in his Declaration hath complained and they do assess the plaintiffs Damages by occasion thereof to one hundred four dollars and eighty three cents. Therefore it is considered that the plaintiff recover against the defendant the damages by the jury assessed and his costs by him about his suit in this behalf expended -

McKee & Cutler)
    vs.)   Debt
James R. Isbell)
          This day came the parties by attornies and thereupon a jury to wit Jacob T. Wyrick, James Biggs, David Rankin, Thomas A. Wilson, Joseph Reader, John Dodd Junr. James Morrow, David Frazier, John Johnson, Casper Easterly, John Dunwoody, John Britton who being elected tried and sworn the truth to speak upon this issue joined upon their oath do say that the Defendant has not paid the debt in the declaration mentioned as in pleading he hath alledged and they do assess the plaintiffs damages by occasion of the Detention of the Debt to twenty five dollars and fifty one cents - Therefore it is considered that the plaintiff recover against the Defendant one hundred and eighty three dollars, the debt in the Declaration mentioned with the Damages by the jury aforesaid assessed and his cost by him about his suit in this behalf expended -
(P-307) Thursday 25th. Octr. 1827

Martin Bailey)
    vs.)   Certio
William Craddick)
         This day came the parties by attornies and thereupon a jury to wit Jacob T. Wyrick, James Biggs, David Rankin, Thomas H. Wilson, Joseph Reader, John Dodd Jr. James Morrow, David Frazier, John Johnson, Casper Casterly, John Dunwoody, and John Britton who being elected, tried and sworn well and truly to try this cause upon their oath do say that they find the Defendant - Therefore it is considered that the plaintiff take nothing by his suit, and that the Defendant recover against the plaintiff his costs by him about his

defence in this behalf expended -

Alexander Laughlin)
    vs.   )   Case
Stephen Alexander)

On motion and cause shewn by affidavit
Jacob T. Wyrick, this cause is continued untill next Court -

Robert H. Wilson)
   vs.   ) Assumpsit
George Smith   )

On motion and cause shewn by affidavit of
Defendant this cause is continued untill next Court -

George Alexander)
    vs.   )   Certio
Andrew Howell)

Continued by consent.

(P-308)   Thursday 25th. Octr. 1827
William Alexander)
    vs.   )   Certiorari Rule to dismiss
John Light   )

This day came the parties by attornies
and thereupon the Rule entered to shew cause why the defendants petition and writ of certiorari should be dismissed
came on for argument. Whereupon all and singular the premises
being seen and by the court fully understood. It is considered
that said Rule be made absolute and that the plaintiff recover
against the Defendant and William Nelson security for the
prosecution of his writ of certiorari the sum of thirteen
dollars and seventy five cents with $12\frac{1}{2}$ pr. cent pr. annum
thereon from the 3rd. day of February 1806 - And also the sum
of ten dollars and fifty seven cents with $12\frac{1}{2}$ pr. cent pr.
annum thereon from the 18th. day of January 1806 being the
amount of two judgments recovered by the plaintiff against
the defendant before Joel Gillenwaters, a Justice of the peace
for Hawkins County at the dates by him about his suit in this
behalf expended -

William Brown   )
    vs.   ) Rule to correct taxation as
Isaac Jones and Mitchael)   to Constables
Bright Security   ) Cost for $7.63 for keeping hogs &c.

This day came the parties by attornies and thereupon the
Rule entered to shew cause why the taxation of costs in this
Suit should be corrected as to witness attendance and constables fees for keeping hogs came on for argument - Whereupon
all and singular the premises being seen and by the Court fully
understood It is considered (P-309) that the Taxation of
costs in said suit be corrected so far as respected the constables costs of $7.63 for keeping hogs &c. and that said
Same be deducted from the Bill of Cost -

State of Tennessee)
     vs.   )   Bastardy
John Keesling   )

      The defendants who stands bound by Recognizance for his appearance here to answer the State of Tennessee of a charge alledged against him for begeting a Bastard child of the body of Ann Hedrick of this County, single woman, was solemnly called for that purpose but came not. Therefore it is considered that the State of Tennessee recover against the said John Keesling the sum of two hundred dollars the amount of his recognizance in this behalf acknowledged unless sufficient cause for such failure be shewn - Philip Harmon who stands bound by recognizance in the sum of one hundred Dollars for the appearance here of John Keesling to answer the State of Tennessee of a charge alledged against him for begeting a Bastard child of the body of Ann Hedrick of this County single woman was solemnly called to bring into court the body of the said John Keesling and surrender the same in discharge of himself as Bail but failed so to do and made default recover against the said Philip Harmon the sum of one hundred dollars the amount of his recognizance aforesaid unless sufficient cause be shewn -

      On motion of the Attorney General ordered by the Court that Scire Facias issue against James Barnes and Securties for a Breach of the Bond given to keep the peace toward all the good people of Tennessee but especially toward Jones Davis -
(P-310)   Thursday 25th. October 1827.

Nicholas Shanks   )
     vs.   )   Ca. Sa. Issued by keeper of
Jacob Hoyal principal)   Justices Records of Greene
John Hoyal and   )   County
John Armitage Securities)

      The Defendant having been arrested by virtue of a Ca. Sa. issued by Alexander Brown keeper of Justices Records of this County at the Suit of the plaintiff on a judgment recovered before Cornelius Newman esquire on the 10th. October 1821 then an acting justice of the peace for Greene County for the sum of fifty dollars and fifty cents debt and one dollar and twenty five cents costs and having entered into bond with John Hoyal and John Armitage Securities continued for his personal appearance here at the present Court to surrender property in discharge of said debt or to take the Benefit of the Insolent Debtors oath as prescribed by the act of assembly and having failed to comply with said Bond - Therefore on motion of the plaintiff by James P. Taylor his Attorney It is considered by the court that the plaintiff recover against the said defendant and John Hoyal and John Armitage his securities for his appearance the aforesaid sum of fifty dollars and fifty cents with Interst thereon from the 10th. day of October one thousand eight hundred and twenty one and his costs in this behalf expended -

      Grand and Pettit Jurrors discharged 3 days.